FRIENDLY INVASION
Memories of Operation Bolero

THE AMERICAN OCCUPATION OF BRITAIN 1942-1945

Officers of the 360th Bomb Squadron, entertain local girls at their Molesworth base, 7 April 1945 (photo courtesy of Mark Forlow)

FRIENDLY INVASION
Memories of Operation Bolero

THE AMERICAN OCCUPATION OF BRITAIN 1942-1945

HENRY BUCKTON

PHILLIMORE

2006

Published by
PHILLIMORE & CO. LTD
Shopwyke Manor Barn, Chichester, West Sussex, England
www.phillimore.co.uk

©Henry Buckton, 2006

ISBN 1-86077-433-4
ISBN 13 978-1-86077-433-1

Printed and bound in Great Britain by
CROMWELL PRESS
Trowbridge, Wiltshire

Contents

LIST OF ILLUSTRATIONS

Frontispiece: 360th Officers party

Acknowledgements

I would like to thank the following for helping with memories, photographs and other information: Deanna Allan, Rosemary Allen, Vera Anderson, Jean Angel, John Astridge, Sylvia Atkinson, Julie Baker, Margaret Ball, Jane Barham, Geoff Bartrum, Vera Bassett, Brian Bawden, Joyce Beard, Jane Bedmanzyk, Mr R.E. Bennett, Olivia Birchell, Tony Blades, Tim Bliss, Mrs M. Borman, Peggy Braybrooke, Mrs Brooks, Mrs J. Bryant, Jack Buzza, Joy Caddy, Roger Carne, Fred Carr, Geoffrey Charge, Margaret Chesterton, Derek Chorley, Paul Chryst, Mrs J. Clarke, Bernice Conway, Enrico Cortese, Mr H. Cox, Betty Currah, Theresa Denton, Eileen Dickinson, David Dodge, Stan Dyer, David Edwards, June Edwards, Derek Evans, Rosemary Farrow, Gladys Fellingham, Joy Ffoulkes, Penny Fleming, Dave Ford, John Gale, Gwendoline Gallech, Bernard Galpin, Mr T.E. Garraway, Beryl Glenister, Gwen Ghijben, Doreen Govan, Bill Gower, Brenda Gower, Mrs B. Grant, Geoff Grater, Cynthia Gray, Hazel Green, Ron Green, John Griffin, Mr K. Grimes, Ronald Grubb, Cyril Guscott, Lomond Handley, Ellice Hansford, Win Harfield, Joe Harlick, Dr David Hay, Mary Hayward, Bunny Hempstead, Mrs A Highley, Whitmal Hill, Peggy Holbrow, Karen Holyoake, Bryan Huxtable, Jim Jefferes, Bryan Keeping, Daphne Kellaway, Gwen Kemp, Frank Kidwell, Dorothy Knapp, Elsie Lewis, Ken Manley, Olive Martin, Jennifer Mason, John Matthews, Joy Matthews, Mrs E. McPace, Roy Mellor, Monica Mercer, Carole Miller, Ann Morley, Pamela Moyse, Mrs V. Mulholland, Muriel Mundy, Pauline Natividad, Anita O'Brien, Colin Osborne, John Owen, Molly Owen, Sylvia Patching, Hilda Paull, Eric Peachey, Rodney Pearce, John Peck, Peter Percy, Walter Percy, Walter Perry, Bernard Peters, Ivor Peters, Sheila Petroff, Sheila Pitman, Bryan Potter, Bob Powell, Eric Puckett, Beryl Reeser, Wendy Rennison, Pat Robinson, Rosemary Robson, Lorna Rundle, Colin Sarel, Mr E.R. Saunders, Annie Sharkey, Alan Shillum, Mary Singleton, Dorothy Smith, Jane Smith, Margaret Sproit, Sheila Stacey, Dorothy Stanley, Mike Stanley, Ivor Strange, Peggy Stephens, Roy Stevens, Sylvia Street, Mrs E. Tamblyn, Peter Tamplin, Daphne Tandy, Lois Taylor, Allan Thomas, Iris Thomas, Patricia Thomas, Jim Timoney, Mrs J. Tombs, Graham Toms, Margaret Topp, Betty Traves, Lorraine Trembath, Gordon Tunnicliffe, Bill Underwood, Bryan White, Joy Wilkinson, Muriel Williamson, and Hilda Willsone.

I would also like to thank Sue Robbins, librarian at the *Gloucestershire Echo*, for allowing me to use research from several of her articles. Tim Grace, 368th Fighter Group Association historian, for his own memories and extracts from the squadron newsletter *The Fortress Feature* written by Herbert Karp. Ruth Wood, reporter for *The Western Daily Press*, for letting me quote from her article about Deborah Prior, and to Deborah herself for her permission. Linda Rarey for letting me reproduce sketches and letters made by her late father-in-law George Rarey, both from the book *Laughter and Tears, The Art of Captain George Rarey*, edited by Damon Frantz Rarey: copyright Damon Rarey; and the website www. rareybird.com created by her late husband Damon as a tribute to his father. Thanks also to Adam Smith, vice president of the Experimental Aircraft Association (EAA) Museum, Oshkosh, WI, for his help with photographs connected to George Rarey. Lindsay Fry for sending me a copy, and letting me use extracts and information published in her father's book *A Teenage View of Weymouth* by Des Fry, printed by The Book Factory, London. Joe Crowfoot for permission to reproduce his paintings, tel. (01502) 715676 www.joecrowfootartist.co.uk. Gary Moncur, from the 303rd Bomb Group Association, for the use of their images, and those of Blanche (Barnes) Gangwere, George T. Mackin and Paul O Harmon. Thanks also to Mark Forlow for the use of his own photographs of the 303rd. Ben Jones for letting me reproduce photographs belonging to www.b24.net. Thanks to Dunkeswell Memorial Museum; Robin Smith 486th Bomb Group Association; Gerry Tyack/Wellington Aviation Museum; Alan Heather/Torquay Museum.

Introduction

Since September 1939 when Britain went to war, its population had faced many impacts and turmoils. The lives of ordinary people were changed in many extraordinary ways. The majority of able-bodied men had been called up by the armed forces, while others that were either too young or too old for active service had joined the Local Defence Volunteers; the ARP; or one of the emergency services. Women of all ages worked in factories and fields, helping to sustain the war effort. Others had joined the armed forces themselves, providing essential back-up services, particularly for the Royal Navy and Royal Air Force. Even children were affected by things such as rationing and evacuation. Then there were the physical dangers that everybody had faced together, during the Battle of Britain and the Blitz. Nearly everybody in Britain was affected by the war in some way.

Then, in 1942, Britain's population faced yet another impact to their lives, as tens of thousands of young American servicemen began to arrive, effectively turning many parts of the British Isles into transit or training camps. Most of these men were in Britain for one of two reasons. They were either part of an infantry, armoured, or airborne division, preparing for the Normandy invasion; or they were airmen taking part in the strategic bombardment of Nazi-occupied Europe, or the Battle of the Atlantic. But whatever their particular reason for being here, their presence over a very short period of time would have a lasting effect on the communities they visited.

This book is not a detailed history of the American occupation of the British Isles during the Second World War, nor the military operations that the Americans took part in, but an examination of the way their presence affected both them and the local people. How friendships and romances were forged between individuals and communities, that existed long after Hitler and his breed had been consigned to dust. It is a social, rather than a military history, and studies the real life experiences of people on the periphery of world-changing events.

But why were the Americans in Britain in the first place and how had they become involved in a second major European war? It all really began on 7 December 1941, when the Japanese made a surprise attack on the US Pacific Fleet, which was anchored at Pearl Harbor. This act of aggression brought the Americans into the war in the Pacific, as allies to the British who were themselves facing a Japanese invasion of Malaya, which ultimately led to the unconditional surrender of Singapore in February 1942.

In September 1940, Japan had become part of the Rome-Berlin-Tokyo Axis. This three-power pact, signed in Berlin, between Germany, Italy, and Japan, meant that the three countries in question would pledge aid to one another for a period of ten years. So, when Japan drew up its plan for the invasion of South-East Asia, which included attacks on the Americans at Pearl Harbor and the British in Malaya, not only did the situation make America and Britain allies, it made America and Germany enemies, as the Germans were allied to the Japanese. On 11 December 1941, four days after Pearl Harbor, Germany and Italy declared war on the United States, shortly followed by US mobilization: the compulsory call up for military service of men between 20 and 44 years of age.

Winston Churchill, the prime minister of Britain, went almost immediately to Washington, to meet President Roosevelt. Both were accompanied by their senior military advisers, and, over lengthy discussions code-named *Arcadia*, these combined chiefs of staff mapped out their plan for global war, with priority given to defeating Germany and Italy. It was agreed that although enough forces should be deployed against the Japanese to hold them in check, no major military operations would take place in Asia, until Hitler, Mussolini, and their regimes had been dealt with. To this end, *Operation Bolero* was set in motion. Bolero was the code-name for the large-scale build up of American forces in Britain.

Planning continued, and the decision was taken to invade North Africa first, followed by southern Europe through Italy, as a precursor to an attack against Hitler's Atlantic sea wall. In the meantime American ground and air forces began to build up in large numbers in the British Isles by mid-1942.

It had previously been difficult and dangerous for convoys to cross the Atlantic Ocean, because of the ever-present threat of German U-boat wolf packs. But by the end of 1942 the balance of power in the Atlantic had begun to shift in favour of the Allies, and it was now possible to transport huge quantities of armour and men across the ocean. Tanks, artillery, and aircraft crossed the pond in preparation for the inevitable invasion of western Europe. And of course, while the members of the many infantry, armoured and airborne divisions set about training, the 8th and 9th United States Army Air Forces (USAAF) were able to enter into the conflict with immediate effect, from bases throughout East Anglia and other parts of Britain. American strategic bombing of continental targets began with the bombing of marshalling yards at Rouen on 17 August 1942.

D-Day, 6 June 1944, was still two years away, when over 70,000 American soldiers participated in the invasion of Normandy from bases in Britain: thousands more would follow in the succeeding months. So for two years, tens of thousands of American servicemen lived and worked in Britain's backyard. Many airmen stationed in Britain remained until the final days of the European war in May 1945. Not only did they live and work in Britain, but they played – and often loved – in Britain as well.

This book is an examination of those eventful and unique years. At no other single time in its history has Britain played host to so many

men and women from another nation. The effect was intense, some
times for the good, and some times for the bad. For many, the effect of
those years of occupation would last a lifetime, and would reverberate
down through the generations that followed.

Chapter 1

'Hey guys, we're in England'

For various reasons American servicemen began to arrive in different parts of Britain from the spring of 1942 onwards. Cheltenham in Gloucestershire was chosen to locate the headquarters of the US Army's Services of Supply Command (SOS). American Army chiefs had insisted on a central site, preferably in southern England, from where they could administer to the needs of the troops and installations that would follow. General John Lee, who had been appointed to command SOS forces in Europe, inspected the suggested site covering Benhall Farm and Oakley Farm in June 1942. The buildings he found there had been built by and for the British War Office, to act as an evacuation point in the event of invasion.

The site proved ideal and, one month after General Lee's inspection, the first wave of US personnel began to arrive. But although office facilities were in place, later occupied by GCHQ, there were no barracks for the men. Officers were quartered in local hotels, while for the GIs tented camps sprang up all around Cheltenham, including one in Pittville

1   American soldiers at a tented camp at Threemilestone in Cornwall in 1944. (Photo: courtesy of Brian Bawden)

2 A B-17 flying over Thorpe Abbots, a typical American airbase in East Anglia. From a painting by Joe Crowfoot. (Copyright: Joe Crowfoot and reproduced with his permission)

Park near the Pump Room, and another at the famous Prestbury Park racecourse. At many locations, these tents were eventually replaced by more permanent forms of accommodation, including brick-built barracks and the now legendary Nissen huts, many of which can still be seen around the country, acting as lasting reminders of this brief moment in our nation's social history.

First impressions

Before long American bases were springing up everywhere, especially in East Anglia, from where the 8th USAAF would begin its bombardment of Nazi-occupied Europe. Throughout the West Country, depots, hospitals and other sites began to appear in preparation for the massive influx of personnel that would arrive during the build up to *Operation Overlord* in June 1944.

To have Americans stationed near your town or village was such a big event, especially for children, that many people naturally always remember their very first contact with them. Many people had a pre-conceived idea of what they were like. As a 14-year-old living in Dereham in Norfolk, Tony Blades had only ever seen Americans at the local picture palace, admitting that he could only associate them with the movie stars he had seen. He and his friends wishfully thought that, back home in the United States, they were probably all either cowboys or gangsters. Impressionable young ladies, on the other hand, might have associated them with the more glamorous type of films they were accustomed to watching, set in places with romantic sounding names like Hollywood, Beverly Hills, or Manhattan.

Dereham was close to several American airbases that had been taken over by men and aircraft of the 8th Air Force – the Mighty Eighth – notably at Shipdham, which had become home to the 44th Bomb Group; and Wendling, where the 392nd Bomb Group had taken up residence. Both of these groups were components of the 14th Combat Wing, and flew a variety of B-24 Liberator bombers during their stay. It was inevitable therefore that, once settled in, the young servicemen who flew and maintained these 'ships', as the Americans called their aircraft, would begin to visit the town.

Tony's first contact happened one afternoon not long after he'd left school and was working in a nearby stationers and newsagent. 'Two Yanks,' he recalls, 'as we affectionately knew them, came into the shop and picked out a picture postcard of the town costing 1d.'

The American showed the card to the teenager, along with a £1 note asking, 'Will this be enough?'. When told that he could purchase 240

3 Meeting the locals. An American soldier chats to a lady walking her dog in Minchinhampton Park, in Gloucestershire, one of the many tented campsites in the area. (Photo: courtesy of Stan Dyer)

postcards for his £1 he said with amazement, 'Gee! Things are cheap in England.'

The prospect of coming to Britain for these young men must have been quite daunting, because, although they largely shared the same language, their culture was very different. In fact, the United States itself is so huge that there were vast cultural differences within its own boundaries. This meant that, as well as coming face to face with the British, they were also meeting American citizens from other parts of the Union for the very first time as well.

Because some of the Americans appeared to be loud, confident, and well paid, compared with British troops, they were generally believed to be men of the world. But in reality, this was often far from the case. For many it was the very first time that they had been away from their homes and indeed for a lot of them the very first time that they had been away from their mothers. This left many of them in a high state of bewilderment, so they were forever looking to be liked by the general populace of Britain. It becomes evident that they did this by being very friendly and over-generous.

Of course there were mixed reactions among the British, who had been at war since September 1939. In Bristol, for instance, Doreen Govan recalls seeing the slogan 'Go home Yanks' appearing in prominent places around the city. 'Rather ungrateful really,' she reflects, 'since the reason they were "over here" was ostensibly to help us win the war.' But for most, there was also a tremendous sense of relief, that at last we had a friend. No longer were the British and her Commonwealth allies fighting alone.

Today, Fairford in Gloucestershire is still associated with the American Air Force, but Jim Jefferes can remember the day when the GIs first arrived. He was in the carpentry classroom at Fairford school, when armoured vehicles began to roll into the town and line up in front of the church. The children were allowed to go outside and watch as the convoy of vehicles, each one bursting with infantry soldiers attired in full battle dress, came to a halt enabling the soldiers to alight.

'This was the tremendous and irrefutable visual evidence that we were no longer fighting the war on our own,' he states, 'but that this huge and powerful country had thrown itself steadfastly behind us. As the tracked vehicles rumbled by the soldiers threw us packs of army field rations. However frugal these rations were, they had a profound effect. For the first time since the beginning of rationing somebody was giving us something freely.'

By four o'clock the town was bustling with American troops and Jim feels that the first impression this gave to the local people was one of positive hope for the future. Their appearance seemed to change the whole atmosphere, as though a dark cloud had somehow been lifted. 'They were friendly,' he says, 'and sympathised with the hardship the country was going through.' Their music and songs touched the imagination and got people singing.

Olive Martin lived in Hampshire near Tidworth Barracks, where during the years immediately before the war she and her family had observed many changes. However, in the summer of 1942 she recalls how this busy place had become completely deserted. Then, one Sunday afternoon, she and her sisters were making their way home from a service at the Methodist church. They knew a shortcut, the route of which took them across the parade square. Suddenly they saw hundreds of men in strange uniforms playing ball games with unusual gloves on their hands. This was their introduction to both the Americans, and their beloved game of baseball.

The military training areas around Tidworth occupied various locations on both sides of the Hampshire/Wiltshire border, but it's probable that the men Olive observed that day belonged to the 29th Infantry Division, who arrived at the barracks in early October 1942.

A little later in the war, the American Army established a camp near the Somerset town of Chard, during the build up to D-Day, at which troops began to arrive in preparation for the invasion of Normandy. Bernard Galpin and his friends would sit and watch the work as the camp was being erected, and recalls an incident which captures the confusion that some of the arriving troops must surely have felt. The men had not been informed of their final destination, and they only knew they had reached it, after arriving.

'I was sitting on a gate at the far end of the camp near a place called Muddy Stile,' says Bernard, 'when a convoy of covered trucks arrived. They stopped, and after a while the backs opened up and out jumped hundreds of troops, looking lost.'

One of the soldiers came across to Bernard to ask where they were? He was told 'Chard', and looked confused. 'Where's Chard?' he furthered. 'In Somerset', was the response. He still looked confused, and after asking where Somerset was and being told, 'In England', he shouted to his pals, 'Hey guys, we're in England!'

In Dorset, the Americans had their eyes on the little village of Charminster, a few miles from Dorchester. Because of its close proximity to Weymouth, which would feature heavily in the American invasion plans, the site was ear-marked as the location for a large ordnance depot, where fighting and other vehicles would be prepared in readiness for D-Day.

In time, the site would become the home and working base for many troops, but Ivor Peters who lived in the village can still remember the day in 1943 when the first Americans arrived. One weekend Ivor and a couple of his pals were walking through the village, when a strange looking lorry came slowly along the road and turned into a lane that led away from the main street. They knew immediately that the vehicle wasn't British. It was painted in a drab khaki colour and the large white stars on the side of the cab and the unfamiliar uniforms of its occupants were obvious clues to its origin.

The boys chased the lorry along the lane and, after it had gone a short distance, it pulled up near the gateway into a large field. Several soldiers jumped out of the vehicle and proceeded to unload a sentry box, which they erected next to the gateway. Having done this, most of the men climbed back into the truck before it pulled away again, leaving behind the sentry box and a solitary soldier armed with a rifle. Ivor explains, 'He was the first American soldier to occupy a site that was to become a large ordnance camp maintaining fighting vehicles, the likes of which we had only seen on the cinema screen.'

But what about the GIs themselves? What was their first impression of Britain? Before the war George Rarey had been a cartoonist and commercial artist. He was drafted into the Army Air Corps and trained as a fighter pilot. He came to England in 1943, and not only kept a cartoon journal of the daily life of his fellow pilots in the 379th Fighter Squadron, 362nd Fighter Group, but sent regular letters home to his recent bride Betty Lou. The consequences of the English weather were often depicted in his cartoons, and his first impression of Britain suitably comes from a letter to his wife sent in November 1943:

> We came down from the Scottish coast on an English train that was a dead ringer for a Hitchcock setting. As we passed through the countryside and villages, the natives gave us a warm and much appreciated greeting. An Englishman on the *Queen Elizabeth* had told us that if we could see the mountains as we approached the British coast, it was a sign that it would soon rain. If we couldn't see the mountains, it was already raining.

Still today, among those who remember the wartime American servicemen who came to Britain, there is a mixture of thoughts, although it quickly becomes evident that many people had pre-conceived opinions long before they even arrived. Many examples illustrate this point, such as the story of Peter Tamplin, who as a boy was evacuated from London to the Isle of Purbeck in Dorset.

Peter was staying at a place called Creech Grange and daily caught the bus to Stoborough Primary School near Wareham, some two miles away. On the day in question he and his companions were running late and consequently missed the bus. Faced with a two-mile trek they were only too glad to accept a lift from a passing US Jeep. 'The Jeep already had three or four occupants,' he explains, 'plus their luggage, so we were perched on top at the back.'

After what he describes as an 'exhilarating trip' they arrived safely at school and only very slightly late. However, on relating the story of their adventure to the teacher, they were given the worst dressing-down of their young lives. For not only had they accepted a lift from strangers, but Americans at that. There was some talk of them having to undergo medical examinations but, after the initial shock had worn off, and the realisation by the teachers that they had not been harmed, the incident was forgotten. 'Bear in mind,' explains Peter, 'that the school was in the hands of aged spinsters.'

Naturally, some of the Americans did live up to their reputation of being brash, and Bill Underwood recalls one occasion when a notable resident of Devizes in Wiltshire was forced into putting bragging Yanks from the 4th Armored Division in their places.

Bill's father ran a barber's shop in Devizes and, when the GIs first began to descend on the town, many would come in for a haircut or shave. One day Jim Jennings, the former mayor, was in the shop waiting for a haircut at the same time as a group of American soldiers. Jim was the owner of fairground rides and noted for his colourful use of the

4 & 5   George Rarey (left) pictured in front of an example of his nose art painted on the cowling of a P-47 Thunderbolt. (Photo: courtesy of the EAA Museum) George Rarey's cartoon, which illustrates his squadron's arrival and disembarkation in Scotland, and subsequent train journey through England. (Illustration: courtesy of Linda Rarey and the EAA Museum)

English language. Bill explains that the vociferous soldiers were both bragging and patronising, saying what a quaint little town Devizes was, and how everything was so much bigger in America.

Eventually, tired of their ranting, Jim Jennings spouted, 'Let me tell you something, this town has the only gas clock in Europe.' He pointed to a clock mounted on the wall of the shop. The clock had been positioned over the end of an old gas pipe, which in the days before the shop had been blessed with electricity, had been connected to a gas mantle. The clock proudly displayed the maker's name, Cole of Devizes and Jim Jennings boasted, 'See this clock, it works on gas and was made in this very town. I'll bet there is nothing like that in America?'

To this day, Bill Underwood isn't sure whether the American soldiers actually believed him or not, but his outburst effectively put them in their place, after which they waited quietly for their turn on the barber's chair.

BLACK AND WHITE

Once an American citizen had signed on the dotted line for the Draught Board, they were informed that they were now 'Government Issue', so these men very quickly became known as GIs. They were also known among the population of Britain as 'doughboys'. The exact origin of this nickname is unsure and, although it had been widely used to describe the men from the USA who fought in the trenches during the First World War, it appears to date back to the Civil War and beyond. However, in Britain during the Second World War the nickname seemed to suit perfectly as, whenever American troops appeared, it wouldn't take long for a vehicle to arrive, both cooking and serving doughnuts to the troops. A number of people also suggest that the nickname was used because of the hats worn by some of the GIs.

Vera Anderson was a teenager during the war years living just two miles from the Knettishall airbase in Suffolk, newly acquired by the 388th Bomb Group with their B-17 Flying Fortresses. The first GIs she remembers seeing were two black military policemen. These policemen, whether black or white, were known as 'snowdrops' because of the white helmets they wore.

Vera's experience of seeing black servicemen first certainly wasn't unique. The reason why this was often the case was because, although black GIs wore the same uniforms as the whites, they were often sent ahead to do manual work with labour battalions, preparing the bases in readiness for the arrival of their white counterparts. Just as the white GIs carried the nickname of 'doughboys', the African American soldiers were often labelled with the derogatory name of 'Jim Crow's Army'.

On the surface this slice of American inequality might not have been realised by the majority of British citizens, who had little understanding of the depth of racism still evident in some sections of American society. To them, America was regarded as the promised land, a place of freedom and equality for all, so they would little suspect or understand what lay beneath the surface.

6   A 'doughboy': Sergeant Al Cunningham. This nickname dates back at least to the Civil War, but the common reason given for its use in Britain was either because of the doughnuts associated with the Yanks, or because of the little hats they wore. (Photo: courtesy of Brenda Gower)

Joy Matthews, who was only nine when the war ended, lived very near the aerodrome at Eye, in Suffolk, sometimes called 'Brome drome', and remembers the arrival of the black American work force, which she describes as being 'shipped in like cattle, to build the dromes'. She doesn't recall any strong racist feelings being expressed by the local people and, in fact, within a short period of time many friendships were forged. 'Once they had done the labouring jobs,' she continues, 'they were shipped off somewhere else.'

In America, there was still a policy of segregation between whites and blacks, which had evidently filtered into the military. Even in major cities there was a strict rule of segregation when it came to things like transport, entertainment and the use of public buildings, and discrimination was widespread when it came to general social attitudes, particularly in education and employment.

When Americans first began to visit Rugby during the evenings, Mrs E. McPace, who worked in a munitions factory, recalls that the whites and blacks would arrive in town at the same time. However, she says, 'All hell broke loose'. There were so many bloody confrontations between the two groups, here as elsewhere, that steps had to be taken to keep them apart. This was achieved in one of two ways, either by giving the groups alternate nights in town or by introducing a form of segregation into the pubs. Using Ipswich as an example, the black soldiers were allowed access to the area around the Cattle Market and docks, while the whites had to stick to the other end of town.

Many of these young men served with units like the 923rd all-black regiment, which arrived in Suffolk in 1942. It must have seemed strange, to come from a segregated society into a community where to a large extent people accepted and welcomed them into their homes. This situation was often harder for the white GIs to accept, many of whom couldn't understand how the British, especially women, could accept black men as their equals. But of course this wasn't always the case, and there was also a certain amount of bigotry towards black soldiers within the British community as well.

Ivor Strange recalls that, just to the east of Dorchester, the park of a large country house called Kingston Maurward was transformed into a massive petrol dump, where black soldiers carried out most of the menial tasks. These soldiers often went into Dorchester on Saturday

7   Mr Gibson of the Red Cross inspects a doughnut-making machine at Molesworth in April 1943. Behind him, on the work surface, a tray of doughnuts can be clearly seen. (Photo: courtesy of 303rd Bomb Group Association/George T. Mackin)

nights for relaxation and the first pub in the area to welcome them was *The Old House at Home* in Fordington High Street, where they enjoyed warm Dorset ales. However, these ales were often very potent and after a few pints one or two of the black soldiers fell foul of Dorchester's criminal fraternity. They would wait in the dark for staggering GIs and 'roll them', the term employed by these local thugs for attacking and robbing them of their wallet, watches, and other valuables.

Ivor's sister Nancy did voluntary work at the forces canteen, which was set up in the Old Wesleyan Church Hall in Dorchester's Durngate Street. This was a place where troops of all denominations, colour and nationality could go if they didn't wish to frequent the pubs.

One night, as Nancy was coming down the steps to walk home to Fordington, her torch failed. It was a pitch-black night, enhanced by the compulsory blackout. She became slightly anxious when three GIs appeared and offered to escort her safely home to Pound Lane. It wasn't until they arrived at the top of the lane that she realised all three of her escorts were black GIs, who after asking with a polite 'are you OK now Ma'am?' headed back to their camp.

Ivor states that: 'If our father had known of this, he would have flown into a rage', underlining the fact that there was a certain amount of bigotry even in his house, which was no doubt typical of the area. As further evidence of this, Mary Hayward provides the following extract from the Norton Fitzwarren Parish Council Minutes, dated 2 October 1944, which clearly show that the parishioners were concerned about the presence of black soldiers on their doorsteps. At Norton Fitzwarren near Taunton in Somerset the Americans had taken over and enlarged what was already a stores depot known as G50.

> Italian Prisoners-of-War and Coloured Troops – After a discussion on the dangers of mixed troops being at liberty to roam our streets and fields at will; resolved to wait a while to see what action can be taken by the military, and in the hope that their stay will not be of long duration.

From this extract, it sounds as though the people of Norton Fitzwarren wanted to have the black American troops incarcerated alongside the Italian prisoners-of-war. No doubt this discussion was born from a desire to keep them off the streets of this quiet Somerset village, and protect the local people from whatever threat they obviously considered them to pose.

As a little girl, Joy Caddy also grew up in Fordington near Dorchester and remembers it being a very busy place during the latter war years. At the time Dorchester was surrounded by American camps, relying heavily no doubt on Kingston Maurward for their fuel requirements. Remember also, that there was a large ordnance camp at Charminster on the other side of the town, so traffic was regularly travelling between the two.

The US Military Police were constantly on point-duty at Fordington crossroads, as lorries, Jeeps and all manner of military vehicles rumbled past the front door of Joy's house. She remembers how these men would occasionally knock on the door, asking to use the toilet, as they were often on duty for long periods of time. Her father, a painter and decorator by trade and wartime special constable, struck up a strong friendship with one of the MPs, a man named John Smith from Cleveland, Ohio, who would always bring him Camel cigarettes.

Joy herself owes a special thanks to one of the black servicemen for teaching her to ride a bicycle. The period in question coincided with the arrival of her first bike, and her mother took her to a quiet road to practise. A passing soldier, seeing that her mother was having difficulties with this task, announced, 'I'll learn her to ride a bike.' Joy goes on to explain, 'and he did!'

Also at this time Joy's parents had taken in a five-year-old evacuee called Johnny. One day the boy said to her mother, 'Auntie can I bring a friend home to tea'. Naturally the reply was, 'Yes dear, of course you can'. Expecting to greet another five-year-old boy from school, imagine their surprise as Joy relates, 'Johnny came in later with the biggest black man I'd ever seen'.

Before 1943, the term 'Colour Bar', hadn't really been used in Cornwall, but it became more common as different elements of the US First Army arrived, and everywhere whites and blacks were accommodated in segregated camps. This situation went directly against the wishes of both President Roosevelt and General Eisenhower (Supreme Commander Allied Expeditionary Forces), who had ordered and issued circular letters to all senior American commanders that there was to be no discrimination or segregation. But however well intentioned this order was, it was basically unworkable. First of all, there was a bigoted attitude among senior army officers, who had a poor opinion of black American troops, believing them to be incapable of combat service. Then of course there were the men themselves, who had a habit of fighting each other, whenever the opportunity arose.

According to Bernard Peters who lived in Truro, the way the black and white GIs were kept in different camps, and had different nights off, astounded local people, who found it puzzling and disappointing. In Truro, the Red Cross had no option but to provide separate clubs, while pubs and other clubs were forced to operate segregation in terms of offering the two groups different nights. He recalls fistfights, stabbings and even shootings, when the two groups were initially allowed to mix. From his memory of the time, Bernard puts the fault mainly down to the white GIs. 'They hated the way our girls took to the black soldiers, and were very surprised that the English did not resent them.'

Although this all paints a very depressing picture of segregation and racial tension, there were certainly instances when white and black GIs were billeted together, and readily tolerated one another. At Gravesend in Kent for instance, the mother of Julie Baker, Mrs Hinkley, who was a young widow with three children and her own mother at home to support, accepted several soldiers into her home. Julie states that, 'the money paid to her was handy'.

At one point Mrs Hinkley had two white Americans staying with her, Corporals Carl Fisher and Seymour Katz, with a third man expected. When the third man arrived, he was first seen at the home of a neighbour, accompanying two other soldiers who were to be billeted at that address. The neighbour's son came rushing in to announce, 'Your American has arrived and he's black'.

Having heard about racial tensions within the army, and the policy of segregation back in the States, Julie's mother became worried about how her other guests would take to this news. She went and spoke to them, explaining about their new housemate, who was a sergeant. When informed of this fact they expressed the view that, 'If he is a sergeant, he must be a good chap'. 'And indeed' agrees Julie, 'he was.'

Sergeant Evans soon became a good friend to the family, helping out around the house, even helping to look after grandma. In fact all three became close friends, but their advice to Julie, who admits to having been a very fussy eater, to eat her vegetables with sweets obtained from the PX club, the American equivalent of the NAAFI, would undoubtedly be frowned upon today.

Back at Knettishall, Vera Anderson goes on to note, that after the black workforce had departed, it wasn't long before the white GIs made themselves known at the airfield, and her first impression of them was being 'full of spirit, quite loud, and very friendly. They were very young, good-looking and wore smart uniforms.' They appeared to have plenty of money and seemed to chew gum endlessly.

'According to them,' muses Vera, 'they all came from Texas.' She thinks this was probably because, in their opinion, the English had only ever heard of Texas. This misconception once again came courtesy of the cowboy movies that were so fashionable at the time. Trying to explain the location of Anoka, Minnesota, or Fayetteville, Arkansas,

8   Black GIs. A group of black soldiers who were camped in fields opposite St Agnes railway station and first came to Mount Hawke in Cornwall to sing in the chapel. (Photo: courtesy of Lorna Rundle)

9   White GIs. A group of First Army soldiers in Yeovil dressed in their walking-out order. They wore the same uniform as the black soldiers, but attitudes towards them were sometimes very different. (Photo: courtesy of Graham Toms)

10   This photograph of crewmen of the 358th Bomb Squadron, dated 9 December 1944, illustrates how young many of the Americans were. For many it was the first time they had been away from their homes and mothers, leaving many in a high state of bewilderment. (Photo: courtesy of 303rd Bomb Group Association/George T. Mackin)

must have seemed like hard work. To some extent she was probably right, and certainly many British children similar to Tony Blades thought of all Americans as being like their favourite Western heroes, and America itself a vast wilderness roamed by huge herds of buffalo. The fact that a high percentage of these young men came from some of the most modern and sophisticated cities in the world would have been unthinkable to a young mind.

A TOUCH OF GLAMOUR

When the first American troops arrived at the village of Broadstone in Dorset in 1943, the local population didn't know what had hit them. The village had already been shaken out of its rather cosy complacency by the arrival of Canadian and French Moroccan troops and the thoughts of Roy Stevens, who lived in the village, give a good summary of the first impressions of many people I have spoken with.

'I remember we invited a Canadian soldier to spend Christmas with us; but the Yanks were something else entirely. They exuded an air of sophistication mixed with a certain degree of charming naïvety, which completely bowled us over. There was an aura of luxury surrounding the ordinary GI compared with his British counterpart. For a start, their uniforms were well cut and of a superior cloth to that of the poor old British Tommy and they wore brown boots with rubber soles and heels – no hobnails! They smoked cigars, chewed gum and seemed to have money to burn. All this, together with their exotic accents, was a devastating blend – especially to the local girls. I remember one American soldier saying to me: "You got any big sisters at home?" I was only nine at the time, and I had to disappoint him.'

The smartness of the uniforms worn by GIs is a recurring theme from numerous accounts. They were not particularly smart as soldiers, marching with a swagger, and often seemed quite casual towards military discipline. They were certainly not the Brigade of Guards, and officers were sometimes known to mess with their men, who they were even heard calling by their Christian names. Such things were rarities in the British Army. But the actual material that their uniforms were made of, their numerous medal ribbons, smart peak caps, and general quality of tailoring, certainly made an instant impression. Officers, with their brown jackets and fawn coloured trousers looked even more glamorous.

In 1942 Bill Gower was serving with the British Army at Colchester, with REME (The Royal Electrical and Mechanical Engineers). His first contact with the Americans happened when he was walking along a public footpath, when he noticed about six uniformed men walking towards him. 'They looked very smart,' he notes, 'and I mistook them for British Army officers.' As the men passed him Bill saluted, but he was surprised when instead of receiving a customary salute in return, one of the men simply said 'Hi!' It was only then that Bill realised his mistake.

At Truro in Cornwall, where there were numerous camps as early as 1943, Bernard Peters explains that the locals knew something was about to happen when a group of Yanks would come outside the railings of their tented camp at Malpas Park, wearing belts and gaiters, with their forage caps tucked under their shoulder epaulettes. They would be chewing, smoking and generally loitering about. Then an officer would appear and instead of calling the men to attention, would say something along the lines of, 'OK guys, dunk them fags, fall in and quit the talking'. Then, once they had fallen in, there were no smart commands of, 'By the left quick march, etc,' which were replaced by, 'OK men, follow me.' As the troop moved off down the road, the only other commands the officer might give would be something like, 'Murphy, spit out that tobacco!'

Doreen Govan's father was particularly unimpressed with the first Americans he encountered one afternoon in Bristol, while walking with his family from Kingsweston Downs to Shirehampton Hill, which had been taken over by the War Department. They came across a camp of young men in lightweight uniforms, soft-soled high-laced boots and what she describes as 'funny-shaped helmets'. Intrigued to discover the identity of the men, her father approached one of them, who was leaning against a wall chewing gum, with his rifle propped up beside him. She recalls how her father returned with a look of disbelief on his face, explaining that the men were 'Yanks', and the one he had spoken with was on sentry duty. Her father had fought in the trenches during the First World War, at which time he spouted the man's attitude would have been 'little short of a hanging offence'.

When the first Americans arrived one bright Sunday morning in the Wiltshire military town of Warminster, to utilise the training areas on Salisbury Plain, David Dodge actually thought the enemy had arrived. He was awoken by the sound of lorries travelling along George Street and, when he and his brother jumped out of bed, pulled up the roller blind, and looked out, they saw a continuous line of army trucks filled with troops wearing what he thought were 'German style helmets!' He was completely dismayed and said to his brother, 'It's the Germans, I thought we were winning the war?'

David goes on to describe his initial impressions of the new visitors, which reiterate the previous point. 'What a change in style, we had been used to the Guards Division regimentally marching through the streets, but these Yanks got about in rubber-soled boots, and chewed gum as they marched – if that was what it was.'

When we consider the American forces that came to Britain during the Second World War, most people have an automatic tendency to think only of young male GIs, but in actual fact, there were also many thousand female military personnel serving here as well. To British women, they must have seemed even more glamorous than their male counterparts; after all they came to grey war-torn Britain festooned with the latest fashions, accessories, and hairstyles.

Throughout the war Eileen Dickinson worked in London as a member of the ATS (Auxiliary Territorial Service) attached to the Royal Corps of Signals. When America came into the war she remembers how the capital was suddenly full of cycling Americans, who came into London during furloughs. During her own limited free time, Eileen and her friends would go to the Stage Door Canteen in Piccadilly, which was an American club open to all service personnel, the original of which had been established in New York City by the USO (United Service Organizations). 'We met GIs there from every state in the USA,' she says. 'There were also a few girls in American uniform as well. I think they were mainly clerks or nurses. I must admit that we ATS girls were slightly envious of their beautiful uniforms and sophisticated manner.' Eileen observed that most of the GIs she came into contact with were very well educated, most of them having come from college. 'They were polite,' she recalls, 'and very interested in visiting all the historical places.'

As already noted, before the war the only Americans that people had seen in the remote villages of England would have been those on the silver screen: people like Clark Gable and James Stewart. So when the glamorous, well dressed, and comparatively wealthy Yanks arrived, they must have all seemed to be like movie stars. In reality, some of them were; both Gable and Stewart, although big stars at the time, volunteered for the Army Air Corps; both also came to England for a short time.

Clark Gable reached the rank or major, and flew five missions over Germany. Almost at the same time that his biggest film *Gone with the Wind* was being shown in the cinemas, he was volunteering to join the army and fight for his country. Many people today still remember Gable in England, and there is much photographic evidence.

One of the most commonly reproduced photos of Clark Gable is from his visit to the 91st Bomb Group at Bassingbourn in Cambridgeshire, talking to the crew of the B-17 Flying Fortress, *Delta Rebel 2*, as it was parked in the 323rd Squadron dispersal area. Whit Hill, who was serving at Bassingbourn with the 91st, explains that Gable, who was a gunnery officer at the time, was giving the *Delta Rebel 2* crew some clues on shooting the 50-calibre machine guns. The *Rebel*'s pilot, Captain George Birdsong, a rather outspoken man, interrupted Gable and asked him to step round to the nose of the aircraft. There painted on the nose was a long double string of yellow Swastikas for each enemy aircraft the crew had shot down. Gable looked at the record, turned around to the group and said, 'I guess I don't need to waste time telling you all how to fire the guns', turned and walked away.

Other stars of the silver screen who served with the American forces during the Second World War included Robert Altman, Ernest Borgnine, Charles Bronson, Mel Brooks, Lee van Cleef, Tony Curtis, Kirk Douglas, Dick Van Dyke, Douglas Fairbanks Jr., Glen Ford, Charlton Heston, William Holden, Burt Lancaster, Lee Marvin, Walter Matthau, Audie Murphy, Paul Newman, Jack Palance, Robert Ryan, Telly Savalas, Rod Steiger, and Robert Taylor. Some of these were already stars, while others became famous in the post-war years, and the majority of them had served in Britain at some point.

But, as well as the Hollywood greats who signed up to fight for Uncle Sam, there were other film stars and singers, who brought their

11   These caricatures by George Rarey of some of the officers in his squadron give a good indication of the relaxed and often casual appearance of American GIs. Even while in uniform they had the ability to look stylish and, to use a modern phrase, 'cool'! (Illustrations: courtesy of Linda Rarey)

glamour to Britain in order to entertain the troops. Celebrities who until then had only been seen in cinemas, visited camps all over Britain and were very much on public view. Personal appearances by people like Bob Hope, Bing Crosby, Jo Stafford, Dinah Shore and Francis Langford all helped to boost the morale of the men, and added a little colour to the lives of people in Britain, who had already been subjected to three years of war. Then of course there are many recollections of concerts given by Glenn Miller and his band, and other swing musicians. Popular American music would fill the air around many bases, as gramophone records were played full-blast over the tannoy systems.

One minor problem was the language difference between the Brits and the Yanks. The English language, as spoken by the Americans,

12 Clark Gable pictured at Molesworth shortly after a combat mission in 1943. (Photo: courtesy of 303rd Bomb Group Association)

had several awkward variations. When in conversation, they would say automobile, gasoline, candy and cookies. The British said motor, petrol, sweets and biscuits. There were a few more sensitive ones too, bum meant a tramp or lay-about, and sitting on your fanny meant backside. They were issued with a booklet explaining this sort of thing – if they bothered to read it. On first arriving in Britain, they also attended classes and seminars on how to behave in front of the natives.

Americans politely called most females 'Ma'am' and the men 'Sir'. The question they asked frequently after they discovered where anyone worked was, 'How much do you make?' This meant how much did you earn? To the British it was a really presumptuous question. The English never asked each other their wage. The GI's didn't mean any offence, but were much more open about such things.

June Edwards, whose family took in American officers while they worked at Bushey Park, the headquarters of the 8th United States Army Air Force, and later Supreme Headquarters Allied Expeditionary Force (Eisenhower's main centre for planning *Operation Overlord*), recalls one officer called Lieutenant Bob Lymann of the Signal Corps. 'He was very tall,' states June, 'and was most impressive in his uniform. After we had chatted a while we decided to go and unpack, my mother thoughtfully being a gracious hostess, asked him what time he would like to be "knocked up" in the morning? There was dead silence and then Bob explained to her that these words had a different meaning in the USA – you can guess what colour her face went!'

On another occasion, when her father was coming home on the tube train, there was a young Polish airman sitting in his compartment with some GIs. After much whispering and pointing, the Polish airman leapt up from his seat and clicking his heels, bowed at a pretty young girl and loudly said, 'Madam you may park your arse here!' This was accompanied by much laughter and sniggering throughout the carriage particularly from the GIs who had obviously coached him in very good English.

From 1942-44, Derek Evans was an evacuee in Desborough in Northamptonshire, a period which to this day he believes still affects his life. One of the house rules at his wartime foster home, was that you didn't go anywhere near the American camp. On contemplation, Derek thinks this rule was in place simply because the family with which he was staying had three daughters, who subsequently became

13 Bob Hope and Francis Langford are among the entertainers visiting Molesworth to put on a show for the troops, 6 July 1943. (Photo: courtesy of Mark Forlow)

14   Movie star Humphrey Bogart visiting Molesworth. Other entertainers in the photograph include Hoagie Carmichael (far left) and Lauren Bacall. (Photo: courtesy of 303rd Bomb Group Association)

like sisters to him. Derek admits that, as a boisterous ten-year-old, he didn't pay much attention to these house rules. Having both a morning and evening paper round, the last drop of which being close to the camp, it wasn't long before he was getting to know the GIs, and taking orders for fish and chips. One of these young GIs acted as a sort of mentor to him, and did eventually become a friend of the family.

'As a child,' says Derek, 'one thing more than anything else has always stuck in my mind. When I entered the hut he would shout out, "No swearing the kid is here!" Imagine a 20-year-old saying that today?'

Chapter 2

HOME SWEET HOME

Many young Americans, particularly in the early days of 1942-43, had come to Britain for a considerable stay; it was therefore imperative that they should feel at home, as quickly as possible. Some of the airbases to which they had been sent were initially built for the RAF, while others were brand new establishments that they largely had to build themselves. They enjoyed various types of accommodation including hotels, wooden huts, bell tents and, perhaps the most famous of them all, the Nissen hut.

However, there is much more to making yourself feel at home than just finding suitable accommodation. The people in Britain and their culture were very different from the GIs, so it was deemed necessary to create an environment where they were able to enjoy as much of their previous lifestyle as possible. In the last chapter, for instance, we mentioned the Stage Door Canteen in London, where GIs were entertained by top American entertainers. This is just one example; all over the area of occupation, Red Cross clubs endeavoured to make the stay of these young soldiers as bearable as possible. It's therefore safe to say that the GIs and their culture had more of an impact on the British than the British way of life had on them.

ALL THE COMFORTS OF HOME

By late November 1943, cartoonist and now fighter pilot George Rarey had arrived with the 362nd Fighter Group at Wormingford, near Colchester in Essex. Here they were accommodated in a type of building which has become almost synonymous with the Second World War. Nissen huts were springing up everywhere and, in a letter home, Rarey gives his opinion of them.

> Nissen as in Nissen hut is merely the name of some misled, well-meaning individual who invented them. A Nissen is a sort of a shelter (at best), sort of like an empty tomato soup can half buried in the mud with a door and two windows at either end. We live in them and scream about them, but they are pretty cozy little deals at that. Our little stove is quite a personality, about three feet high and ten inches across, cylindrical in shape. There is a small opening in the top to put in coal and an equally small opening in the bottom to take out ashes. On the surface this coal-to-ashes cycle sounds quite simple. But not so. The stove is not equipped with a grate and successful operation requires patience and cunning with a dash of luck.

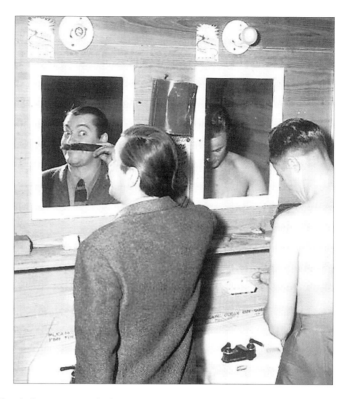

15 USO entertainer Jerry Cologna uses the washing facilities at Molesworth in 1943. (Photo: courtesy of 303rd Bomb Group Association)

Nissen huts had first arrived during the First World War and were the dream-child of Peter Norman Nissen, whose Norwegian father had emigrated to the USA during the gold rush. Peter later moved to Britain and joined the Royal Engineers, where in late 1916 his invention was finalised. In order to accommodate troops, these early prefab huts could be easily and quickly constructed, all the components of which could be transported on the back of a lorry and assembled by six men in a few hours. Their semicircular shape and coating of corrugated iron gave them the ability to deflect shrapnel and bomb blast, which made them perfect bomb shelters as well. This made them ideal, not only as accommodation, but for use as stores, hospital wards, training rooms, messes, and for a great many other military purposes.

When the personnel of the 368th Fighter Group, 9th USAAF, arrived at Newbury in Berkshire on the wet English morning of 13 January 1944, their convoy of trucks eventually stopped just across the county border, in the midst of what seemed to be 'a long row of overturned ash cans'. This description was made by Sergeant Herbert Karp, who wrote an account of the episode for the group's self-published newspaper *The Fortress Feature*.

These 'ash cans' of course, were Nissen huts destined to be their homes for the next couple of months. 'The Company Street,' he wrote, 'was muddy, the sky was gray, and it was drizzling slightly. It wasn't pleasant at all, but it lived up to what we had heard and read about English weather. We spent the first few days doing little more than adjusting ourselves to the country, the living conditions, the money and the blackout. A total blackout was in effect and by six each evening it was pitch dark. Those unfortunates who had no flashlights found themselves grasping their way in the darkness, going to and from the barracks, and very often ending up in the bushes along the road.'

Before long, this period of rest and relaxation was over, and Herbert Karp and other personnel were daily ferried to work at Greenham Common, where, as part of the 71st Fighter Wing, they operated P-47 Thunderbolts. The airfield was just across the county border on top of a hill, which had been a golf course before the war. Thus, although Newbury and Greenham Common where they worked were in Berkshire, the camp where they slept was in Hampshire. The 368th were stationed on one side of Greenham Common, while on the other side of the field was a place that became known as Shantytown.

'Shantytown' continued Mr Karp, 'was the name affectionately given to the living area of the men of a glider assembly outfit. After taking the gliders from the boxes and assembling them, they converted the glider boxes into living quarters, and very comfortable ones at that.'

The gliders these men assembled would later play an important role in the invasion of Nazi occupied Europe, while the crates they arrived in became a popular form of temporary shelter, much in demand at other bases, even those at which no glider troops were based. Similarly, at other bases including Wendling, shacks were built from old bomb crates.

At USAAF Station 121, Bassingbourn in Cambridgeshire, home of the 91st Bomb Group, things were quite different. Built just before the war, the airbase at Bassingbourn had been the show place of the RAF. All buildings except the hangars boasted central heating, and it became known amongst the Americans as 'the Country Club'. Whitmal Hill, who served with the 91st, explained that the barracks even had hot and cold running water in the bathtubs and showers.

The American set-up at Bassingbourn required the use of land owned by a large country house, called Wimpole Hall, which is today owned by the National Trust. Much of the land was used as parking bays for the group's B-17 bombers. In fact, some of the best-known individual aircraft of the Second World War were flown from here: including *Nine-O-Nine*, which flew an amazing 8th USAAF record of 140 casualty free missions; and perhaps the most famous of them all, *Memphis Belle*, the crew of which were the first to complete 25 bombing missions, all of which were flown from Bassingbourn.

At the time in question, Whitmal Hill thinks that Wimpole Hall was owned by a Mrs Bambridge, of whom he says, 'I guess she was on our side during the war, but probably put out that the government took part of her property for a B-17 parking place. On another section of the property there was established the Arrington USAF Military Hospital. I only saw the dear old lady twice, and she was waving a cane and telling me to get off her property. I do believe, however, that she did invite some of the officers over for a dinner or tea, but I am not sure.'

Going to work each day, Whitmal Hill was impressed by the giant elm trees that lined the parking strip. The trees ran parallel, from near the house to the Royston/Huntingdon road, and pointed towards the main Bassingbourn runway. Pilots returning from a mission, especially in lousy weather, were always glad to see Wimpole Hall and its line of trees.

Having been spoiled at the Bassingbourn airbase, with such luxuries as hot and cold water, Mr Hill found things a bit more primitive at the parking bays at Wimpole Hall, where he worked on the parked aircraft. For a start there was no running water on the site and, until they acquired a few of those much sought-after glider crates, there was no place for the airmen to shelter from the English rain and, of course, the cold and snow during the winter.

They did have outdoor privies, one of which was chosen by a certain master sergeant as his favourite. Unfortunately, the one he picked stood close to the tail of a parked B-17, which led to some high jinks. 'The Sergeant had rather regular habits,' explains Whitmal Hill, 'and on the days the plane was stood down, for some reason or other, the assistant crew chief and I would get up in the cockpit and watch for his arrival. By the time he had gotten his pants down, we had the engines running. The out house door faced the aircraft (I think it was *The Careful Virgin*), and we would run the props up and try to blow it over. The wind force was so strong he couldn't open the door. After a few moments we would shut the engines down and watch for him to come out in a rage. If he went for the tail door, we would escape out the nose hatch, jump on our bikes and take off. He never did catch us, and I don't think he had a clue who we were. Hell, one had to create his own amusement in those days.'

16   Huddled around the stove; George Rarey's impression of the inside of his Nissen hut at Wormingford. (Illustration: courtesy of Linda Rarey and the EAA Museum)

Eventually tiring of this prank, they moved on to something else, slightly more dangerous: dropping a 50-calibre cartridge into the potbelly stove that was in the glider crate they used to keep warm in. 'It was one sure way to get a place near the stove.' The cartridge usually went off with just a bang, but the practice stopped when one got jammed in the fire pit, and blew a small hole in it.

Another way to make yourself feel at home is to have a dog, and before long Americans at bases all over East Anglia had acquired quite a considerable menagerie of assorted canine companions. George Rarey's Nissen hut at Wormingford was cheered up by the presence of Bruno, who he describes in a letter to Betty Lou dated 6 December 1943.

'We bought a little black dog from an English laborer. He is a cute little rascal, good-looking in a nondescript canine way. He immediately went AWOL for about 10 days. Tonight he showed up again. We've decided to waive the court-martial and give him another chance. He was glad to see us and seems a trifle sheepish. I asked him where he'd been, and as he didn't answer, I must assume it was some carnal orgy. I told him that his sordid little love life didn't interest me in the least, and casting me an evil leer, he took over my sack – he's over there now, corking it off. Move over, Bruno, you bastard!'

At Reen Cross Farm, about a mile from Perranporth in north Cornwall, it was Bob the dog who befriended the Americans who at that time were camped along the lanes during the final weeks before D-Day. Ronald Grubb's father Arthur owned the farm, and Ronald recalls an incident when troops were marching past and Bob decided to march after them. He was eventually returned to the farm sitting on the back seat of a Jeep. 'This happened on more than one occasion,' muses Ronald.

In the Blackdown Hills at Hemyock in Devon, John Griffin supplied American Naval personnel with another sort of pet. Hemyock was very close to the US Navy's airbase at Dunkeswell, where men of the Fleet Air Wing 7 flew PB4Y-1 Privateers on anti-submarine patrols in the Atlantic. The PB4Y was the Navy's version of the B-24 Liberator. As a boy, growing up in Hemyock, Mr Griffin belonged to the Rabbit Club which bred Flemish Giants, a breed noted at the time for its meat-producing quality, and for which he was allowed a ration of feed.

'American servicemen in quality uniforms would swagger down Station Road past our house,' he recalls. 'We received about half a crown for each rabbit from the Club but the Yanks gave us a pound. I don't think they ate them because their mess rations were so good. I like to think they were kept as mascots and pets.'

During the latter stages of the war, there were so many American servicemen descending on the West Country that improvised accommodation was essential. As well as the Nissen huts already mentioned, people became familiar with the sight of camps brimming with hundreds, if not thousands, of their famous six-man pyramidal tents, all lined up in neat rows, with smoke gently rising from their centre stoves. Tented camps appeared everywhere during the build up to D-Day, and it has been suggested that, in those final weeks, the American Army actually outnumbered the local population.

17   Ground crews work on their aircraft at Bassingbourn. In the background is the local chicken farm, where the men obtained fresh eggs. (Photo: copyright Paul Chryst)

THE RED CROSS

When the 368th Fighter Group first arrived at Greenham Common, the men did their best to make themselves feel at home under very difficult circumstances. But no immediate facilities had been put in place to cater for their relaxation and entertainment. A representative of the group therefore made arrangements with the women of the Red Cross who were working on the station, to remedy the problem. Tim Grace, the group's association historian, provides the following account from 396th Squadron documents:

18   B-17 Little Patches, one of the 91st Bomb Group's Flying Fortresses, is 'revved up' and ready to taxi from its dispersal area at Bassingbourn. (Photo: copyright Paul Chryst)

19   George Rarey's drawing of the arrival of Bruno. (Illustration: courtesy of Linda Rarey and the EAA Museum)

On 15 January the lounge and library in the Aero Club opened. They served coffee and sandwiches from the Enlisted Men's mess hall. All sat in front of the fire, talked and sang. It did help the spirits of the men. On special evenings, the Aero Club served cakes, coffee and free snacks from the un-rationed foods until the snack bar could be opened. Miss Florence Reed was the charming Red Cross representative who did all she could for the boys' entertainment. January 21st brought the first dance with most of the girls who attended the affair coming from nearby branches of the Women's Land Army. The men from the Squadron eagerly attended, and thereafter made sure of trying to be present at all the affairs which the Aero Club tendered. Our own Sgt. N. Fowler, who hails from the state of Tennessee, came down to the club some evenings with his guitar and entertained by singing songs, some of the lyrics and tunes being very typical of his native home state. He is always a hit with the men and the girls.

Two officers from Special Services were assigned to the group, who endeavoured to screen American movies whenever possible. These films were a big hit, much appreciated, and during the afternoon of the scheduled days, the camp would reverberate with the words, 'Hey fellas, let's get to chow early, there's a movie tonight'.

On 15 March 1944 the 368th left Greenham Common for Chilbolton, from where they would launch their P-47 Thunderbolts into the war, as part of the 71st Fighter Wing. The Nissen huts they were accommodated in at Chilbolton were the same type as before, and Special Services continued to administer to the recreational needs of the men. To ensure continuity, they got to work immediately on the Aero Club, in order to have a head start for when Miss Florence Reed arrived to continue her efforts for the Red Cross.

One of the British Red Cross contingent who remembers Florence Reed at Chilbolton was Win Harfield. She remembers vividly how aircraft and gliders would train daily from the airfield before the

20   American Red Cross girl Mary Croft, with two of the lads in front of the American Red Cross Club at Chilbolton. (Photo: courtesy of Win Harfield)

invasion of France. They practised continually, she recalls, circling around before the aircraft released the glider, by dropping the towrope. Once, a towrope from one of these aircraft sliced through the chimney of a neighbour's bungalow in Station Road, Chilbolton.

At the time Win was living with her parents in Chilbolton, while her husband was away serving in the Royal Tank Corps. They had a small son called Christopher. When the Americans opened their Red Cross club, they advertised for part-time workers to make their famous ring doughnuts. Her mother agreed to care for Christopher, enabling her to apply for the job, which she got, along with one other lady. They were provided with the flour and cutters needed to craft the doughnuts: 'The boys loved them,' she proudly claims.

The club was run by two American girls: Florence Reed was the manageress from Seattle, and Mary Croft, who Win believes hailed from New England. There was also a padre, Father Cleary, who supported them and seemed to be almost a father figure to many of the lads, especially if they had any problems. All costs for running these clubs were met by the American people. The area manager, also an American, was Mr Dworran, who was stationed at Bournemouth. After a few months, however, they were informed that the doughnuts would in future be made at Greenham Common and delivered to Chilbolton daily. So having enjoyed her short period of employment, it seemed that Win was about to lose her job again, which worried her as she was trying to save as much money as possible towards their future home. However, on the final day, to her surprise, Florence called her into her office and told her that they were now looking for a manageress to run the business side of the Chilbolton club. Having only worked for an insurance company previously Win didn't feel qualified for the job on offer, but Florence was adamant that she had all the necessary qualities:

besides she would be there to offer her support. The hours were longer, but the salary was good, so she discussed it with her mother and finally said OK.

It was decided to employ local ladies to do the cleaning etc., so one of her first jobs was to interview, with Florence, ladies of various ages from the village. This was a daunting prospect, as some of the ladies had known Win all her life, so perhaps they would resent being told what to do by a youngster. Her way of dealing with this situation was to always ask the ladies to do something, rather than order them to do it: 'Bless them,' she says, 'they were wonderful.'

The work force was picked up each day by a Jeep and ferried to the club, where they had to remain during their working hours, as no civilians were allowed to roam the camp. Win herself was the exception to this rule and would accompany Florence to the officer's mess for lunch. 'The officers,' she explains, 'and ourselves queued up and selected our meals from a wonderful array of dishes. How I wished I could take my lovely lunch home sometimes for the family.'

One of Win's duties was to take the cash once a week to the bank with a Jeep and driver supplied. On one occasion Florence came with her, and offered to carry the bag of cash. On the way they stopped to do some shopping, and it wasn't until they arrived at the bank, that Florence realised she had mislaid the bag. 'I panicked,' states Win, 'but Flo was her usual unfazed self. We retraced our steps, and eventually found the missing bag, reclining on the counter in Woolworths.' Win recalls that it had been a busy day, so many people must have noticed the bag on the counter, which contained over £500!

21   Elsie Lewis standing outside the American Red Cross Service Club, in Devizes, where she worked. (Photo: courtesy of Elsie Lewis)

22   Card presented to Elsie Lewis (née Caswell), on appointment as a hostess at the American Red Cross Service Club in 1944. (Photo: courtesy of Elsie Lewis)

AMERICAN RED CROSS DONUT DUGOUT.

AMERICAN RED CROSS IN GT. BRITAIN.

This is to certify that

Miss Elsie Caswell.

has been accepted as Hostess at the Devizes Service Club.

Date..7..10.44..   Isabella Meali.

23   Members of staff and American soldiers at the American Red Cross Club in Devizes, Wiltshire. (Photo: courtesy of Elsie Lewis)

All went well until the end of the month when Win had to produce a statistics report, to send to Mr Dworran, which she simply couldn't get the hang of. However, help manifested itself in the shape of a man called Ernie. At the time, there were several RAF personnel working on the base, who had been downgraded for medical reasons. These men began to complain that they had no club or NAAFI for themselves. Win took their case up with Florence, who explained that it was a difficult situation because these Red Cross clubs were paid for by public subscription in America, for the use of 'their boys'. She promised to see Mr Dworran who came up with the suggestion that, if the RAF lads were willing to give a few hours of their time to help out in the club, they would be welcome to use it socially at other times. One of the lads in question was Ernie, who had experience of statistics, and he volunteered to do a rough draft of the report for Win, which she believes saved her job.

'Sometime later,' she continues, 'Ernie had a message that his home in Kent had been bombed. His wife and two sons were OK, but homeless. So Ernie went on leave, and Flo told Mr Dworran what had happened. He set wheels in motion, and when Ernie eventually returned, Flo came into the office and with a big smile on her face, she said "I have a job for you. Please give this to Ernie." She handed me an envelope with a cheque in it. I don't remember the value, but I know it was several hundred pounds. Ernie wept and I wept with him, what a couple of fools we must have looked.'

Win thought the Americans 'were great' and when her husband returned home on leave from the North African battlefields, where he had been fighting with Montgomery's Eighth Army, the GIs were eager to meet him. 'They were very impressed with a veteran,' she states, 'and asked him all sorts of questions. I realized then just how young and scared some of them were.'

One morning Win was greeted by Florence with the news that the boys had gone. Although her mother's house was only yards from the airfield, they hadn't heard a thing, which she assumes was simply because they had become so accustomed to the sounds of the men training, that the noise as they moved out hadn't registered.

The club prepared to close and Win was allowed to keep one of her ladies on while an inventory was made, before all remaining contents were transferred to Middle Wallop. Florence Reed in the meantime was told that she would be flying to France to set up a Red Cross club for their lads as soon as possible. She immediately came up with the idea that Win should accompany her for a few weeks to get the club started.

Poor Win got herself in a bit of a state: it would be exciting but would it be dangerous? She didn't want to let Florence down, but what would her husband think, let alone her mother and small son? Florence was convinced that the situation would only arise if the area in which the club was to be set up, was safe. She put her plan to Mr Dworran, and the eventual reply was to the effect that, although the Americans would allow it, the British were not prepared to risk their civilians in such a way. Win was relieved that the decision had been made for her, admitting that it would have been a very difficult choice to make.

When Florence Reed eventually flew to France, Win saw her off, and was horrified to see that her journey would be spent sitting on the floor of a transport plane. She suffered from airsickness, so before her departure consulted the MO, who gave her some tablets to take two hours before take off. She followed these instructions, taking the pills at the required time, only for the flight to be postponed, which meant that when the flight did eventually get airborne, their effect had worn off.

In time Win received a letter from Florence, saying that the club was nearly ready and that she had met up with some of the boys. Even Father Cleary was there, who had taken to towing an altar behind his Jeep and, ignoring enemy action, would hold impromptu services wherever he could.

One other point that Win stresses was that no alcohol was ever served at these Red Cross clubs, so the men who used them regularly did so in preference to hunting out local pubs. 'I found these lads all really nice,' she states, 'some liked teasing and making fun of we English girls, but they mostly wanted to talk about their homes and families.'

The Red Cross played an important part in helping to make the visitors feel at home. Some of the Red Cross ladies, such as Florence Reed and Mary Croft, came with the troops from America, while others, like Win Harfield, were volunteers within the communities to which they were sent. Another such volunteer was Elsie Lewis who found herself working in the American Red Cross canteen on The Green in Devizes, Wiltshire. The 4th Armored Division were based in the area and, after they left on D-Day, the staff changed the name to the 'Donut Dugout'.

'I helped to make thousands of doughnuts,' says Elsie. 'The American girls we worked with were great.' Her boss at the canteen was called Ruth Drusken, who must have been happy in her work, because Elsie has vivid memories of her coming into the kitchen every morning singing 'Mersey Dotes and Dosie Dotes.'

Elsie also remembers wonderful dances and making many friends, both male and female. For a while she was going out with a young soldier in the finance group called Mike Monez, but following D-Day she didn't hear from him again, presuming he had been killed. That was until 1978, when she had a phone call from America, because Mike was attempting to trace her. By then he had been married, divorced, and had four children. They are still in contact today.

Sylvia Atkinson worked as the receptionist in the American Red Cross Officer's club at Minster House in Winchester, where the director was a Miss Crowther. She got to know several Americans quite well, particularly those who worked in the kitchen: George, the Austrian pastry cook, she recalls made the most wonderful apfelstrudel; Tony, a merry little Italian; and Johnny, a southerner with suitable accent. 'All went to Normandy,' she says. 'None of them survived.'

She was only 18 but clearly remembers the part the Red Cross played: 'We held regular dances at the club. There were even a couple of weddings at which an American padre officiated. GIs were also invited to civilian homes on a regular basis. In our own home, despite the strictures of rationing, we regularly had American servicemen as guests. One thing that endeared them to us, and to my mother in particular, was their impeccable manners.'

ROOM AND BOARD

With so many men to accommodate, there were various schemes in place to house them, but in some instances American personnel moved in with British families. For the British themselves this was nothing new as, since the outbreak of the Second World War, many had accepted evacuees into their homes.

One such officer was Bob Powell, who on arriving in Britain went to Atcham in Shropshire for continuation training as a fighter pilot. After leaving Atcham, he joined the 352nd Fighter Group based at Bodney in Norfolk, with whom he had completed two combat tours, flying 87 missions, first in P-47 Thunderbolts and later in P-51 Mustangs. At the end of his

24   Troops on a training exercise gather around a Red Cross Clubmobile, offering refreshments. (Photo: courtesy of Brenda Gower)

two tours he was due for rotation back to the US. However, because someone with his newspaper experience was required for a vacancy at Bushey Park, Watford, the HQ of 8th USAAF Fighter Command, he found himself in Hertfordshire, remaining until December 1944, when he finally received orders to rotate back home.

During this time he was billeted with the Edwards family, who lived in Silverdale Road, Bushey, which was just a short walk from Bushey Hall. 'We had our own mess hall,' he says, 'and we took our meals there, but the officers were housed with British families under the Lend Lease agreement with the US. I don't know the details, but these families were financially rewarded for taking us in.'

The Edwards family were: father John, mother Emily, and two daughters June and Margaret. The house had four bedrooms, two bathrooms, and five downstairs rooms including a music study, which Mr Edwards had made bomb proof, by reinforcing it with timber on the inside, and by building an additional brick wall on the outside.

'Anyway,' continues Bob Powell, 'the Edwards family were very nice to me and I enjoyed the opportunity, to experience living with a British family and being "accepted" by them almost as a member of the family.'

Mr Edwards worked for the London Midland and Scottish Railway, and was responsible for keeping lines of communication open between all the railway stations from the south coast to Coventry, and the Midlands beyond. This meant there were many phone calls at night following air raids and, for the family and their American guests, many sleepless nights, as well as a certain amount of stress. John Edwards also did local fire watch duties.

When time permitted Bob Powell played tennis with the girls at two privately owned courts nearby, but he says that they were 'too young at that time to have a romantic relationship'. June was 16-17 years old, and Margaret 14-15; and anyway he had a sweetheart back home. He also spent long evenings with the family talking about America and what the Americans thought of 'jolly ole England'.

25 American Red Cross Clubmobile visiting the 303rd. It was always welcome with its coffee, doughnuts and conversation with pretty Red Cross girls. (Photo: courtesy of 303rd Bomb Group Association)

26   American Red Cross Clubmobile parked in front of the B-17E *Phyllis*, which was assigned to the 303rd Bomb Group Headquarters and used for formation assembly and tow target work. It was the only B-17E at Molesworth. (Photo: courtesy of 303rd Bomb Group Association)

'Needless to say,' Bob states, 'I fell in love with England and its people. I found some a little hard to know, possibly because of what they had been told about the "Yanks", or maybe what they had observed. But being a hillbilly from West Virginia, I never met a stranger, so to speak. My wife always says I didn't have any problems because I could "talk to a rock".'

While staying with the Edwards family, Bob remembers that the family's rations were only about two ounces of meat, per person, per

27   This painting by Roger Lane shows a B-24 Liberator flying over East Anglia on a winter's day. (Reproduced with the permission of Roger Lane)

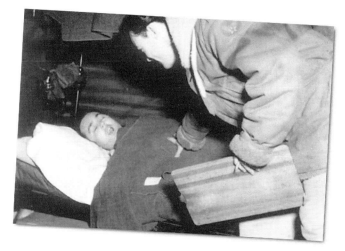

28 T/Sgt Alexander Hartmann in bed at Molesworth, being woken up for an early mission. (Photo: courtesy of Mark Forlow)

week. At the mess hall where he ate, most Americans consumed more than that at each meal. So it must have been quite disturbing each day to have gone from a world of relative plenty, back to his billet where the local people were still heavily rationed. This situation led to one of his most endearing memories of the Edwards family, and perhaps illustrates a trait of the British character of the time.

'When I told Mr and Mrs Edwards that I would soon be getting orders to return to the US, they secretly refrained from enjoying their meagre meat ration and other foods, to put enough aside to invite me to a farewell dinner with them, in their home. What wonderful, generous, loving people.'

So what could Bob do to show his appreciation for their sacrifice? As he was a non-smoker, he took all of his cigarette rations to the mess sergeant at his own mess hall, and exchanged them for beef, which he then presented to the Edwards family as a farewell present. Bob married his high school sweetheart Betty on 4 January 1945, after returning home on Christmas Eve, but through the succeeding years has occasionally corresponded with the Edwards family.

But Bob Powell was only one from a string of American officers who spent time at the house in Silverdale Road. June Edwards recalls that the house was only a few streets away from Bushey Park, which had previously been a golf and country club. The main building was turned into the administration offices and mess for the officers. Nissen huts were built for the enlisted men and a guardhouse constructed at the entrance.

'There were lots of Jeeps roaring up and down Aldenham Road,' writes June, 'much to the annoyance of cranky residents and the recruits of a Coldstream Guards battalion who were in an empty large house – which they wrecked. They were jealous of the GIs, their uniforms and their rate of pay, which was much more than they were receiving. Bob Hope and his gang, and also Glenn Miller and his band all performed at HQ.'

As mentioned by Bob Powell, her mother had to cope with very meagre rations, allowed only two ounces per week of the following

29   At the morning briefing, and T/Sgt Alexander Hartmann, on the right, still doesn't look totally awake. (Photo: courtesy of Mark Forlow)

items for each member of the household: meat, butter, cheese, sugar, and tea. There was no bacon or fresh eggs, only powdered eggs. Milk was also powdered, except for one pint each a week. Apples were the only available fruit, as nearly everything else at that time was imported. But her father had a victory garden, in which he was able to grow lots of vegetables. But the lack of tea, in her words, 'was the worst'.

Among the other American officers who stayed with the Edwards family were Lieutenant Robert Woody from Roanoke, West Virginia, who remained with them for some considerable time. He was a fighter pilot, decorated for bravery in Okinawa. On one occasion a mechanic at his airbase, having received a 'Dear John' letter from his girlfriend and intending to commit suicide, took up a plane. Bob Woody flew his own aircraft skilfully beneath the man, thus defusing the situation, and eventually he managed to talk him down. The boy in question was court-martialled, but later became a pilot himself.

Then there was Bill Busch, who served with an Eagle Squadron. These were American pilots who flew with the RAF before the US officially entered the war. Sadly, Bill was killed just before his tour of duty finished, and June remembers the sadness felt by the family when the billeting officer came to collect his belongings.

Colonel Hunkere had been at Pearl Harbor with his wife. After the Japanese attack, he had lost contact with her for almost a week, until she returned with their servants, having escaped to the safety of the surrounding hills. After the war, both Lieutenant (later Colonel) Woody and Colonel Hunkere returned to England, and visited the Edwards family.

30   A B-24 Liberator of the 392nd Bomb Group based at Wendling. (Photo: courtesy of www.b24.net)

31   While he was living with the Edwards family, Bob Powell would return to the American mess hall for most of his meals. This photograph shows the sergeants' mess at Molesworth, although, as the caption reads '358th Bomb Squadron Banquet', normal sittings wouldn't have been quite so grand. (Photo: courtesy of 303rd Bomb Group Association/George T. Mackin)

Another officer to stay with them, June recollects, 'was Major Farnsworth, who I think came from Alabama and told many interesting stories of his family's cotton plantation and the slaves that were owned by his grandfather. Apparently they didn't want to leave when they became free people, so they stayed on as servants.'

Then there was Captain Stangel. 'He was absolutely charming,' admits June, 'but unfortunately had three wives in England and a current girlfriend who we had met – the military police arrived one day and escorted him away – what a guy!'

The Edwards family got along with all their American guests. There was only one officer that John Edwards got a little upset with, as he would bring his revolver, flak jacket and helmet down in the evenings, and proceed to clean his revolver on the dining room table. He was finally told to clean his weapon in his own room and, if there wasn't an air raid on, 'why on earth did he need his tin hat anyway?'

In Southgate Street, Bury St Edmunds, Bryan Potter recalls that his parents rented out their best front room to an American captain called Jack and his wife Elsie. He recalls them being 'a lovely couple', which was probably enhanced by the fact that Jack somehow managed to acquire a superb balsa wood kit of a Spitfire that he duly presented to the young Bryan as a gift. With roughly a 12-inch wing span, the model was far superior to anything he had previously come across among the few model kits available in town. And, being a keen modeller at the time, he was thrilled by the challenge of building and painting it.

Elsie and Frederick Everitt, the parents of Bernice Conway, had two GIs billeted with them at their house in Fairfield Place, in Southville, Bristol. The first of these was Ferdinand Kuchman from New York State. He must have written to his family about the Everitts who received several food parcels from them. On leaving, he was replaced by Roald Neprud, who eventually left on D-Day plus one.

From childhood, Bernice's clearest memories of these men were the evenings when she was sent to knock on their door, and announce that supper was ready. 'It must have been a shock to them at first,' she jokes, 'supper was a cheese sandwich: the cheese as tough as iron and a cup of cocoa made with water. But if they didn't enjoy the food, they did enjoy the conversation and family atmosphere.'

Her saddest memory is of standing at the front door next to Roald, waiting for the truck to arrive on the day of his departure. Up and down the street, other families were saying goodbye to their own resident GI. 'It was very quiet after they left,' she recalls, 'and most of the women were in tears.' They never heard from Roald again, although they did hear from a married Frederick, who Bernice visited in the 1960s. She remembers both being decent young men, 'never brash and noisy, as usually portrayed'.

Margaret Topp was 11 years old when a dashing young lieutenant came to join her family and share their home. Lieutenant William (Bill) Uhl and his fellow officers were stationed at the Southern Command Headquarters at Wilton near Salisbury, which is where the family lived at the time. All the officers were billeted in private accommodation, and Margaret says, 'It certainly helped our financial situation.'

When Lieutenant Uhl first came, as well as his own bedroom he was given a private lounge, but quickly turned this down as he wanted to be treated like one of the family. 'And he was,' explains Margaret, 'for over three years.'

Bill shared everything with the family, and his own mother and family were always so grateful for what they did for him that they sent many parcels of food, clothes, and linen etc. Margaret still has a doll she was sent, to add to her many happy memories.

32   Catholic chaplain Father Edmond Skoner of the 303rd Bomb Group conducts a mass, at what would appear to be a pre-mission briefing at the flight hut. (Photo: courtesy of 303rd Bomb Group Association)

33 This painting by Roger Lane, titled 'The Sound of Thunder', illustrates perfectly how, in spite of the presence of the Americans in East Anglia, life went on for the ordinary working people, particularly those engaged in agriculture. (Reproduced with the permission of Roger Lane)

After Bill returned home, by which time he was a captain, he married and went on to have four children. But he and his family always kept in touch with his wartime friends and, 47 years later, Margaret visited them in Indianapolis, after learning that Bill was going blind.

'Strangely,' she writes, 'I recall that whilst in Bill's home I saw some lovely pictures of Rothenburg, Germany, on the wall and, so commenting, was told Bill's father came from Germany as mine did! Imagine my surprise years later, when visiting my cousin in Germany, I was taken for the day to Rothenburg and spotted a Bakery called Uhls.' Bill and his wife have both since died, but Margaret still keeps in contact with all their children.

Molly Owen was a schoolgirl living in Wingfield Road, Lower Knowle, Bristol, when American troops were based at Victoria Park, and most of them were billeted on the people in the local area. As both her brothers were away in the British Army, her family had two Americans billeted with them, and she remembers vividly the day they arrived. 'I had just come home from school. There was no one else at home, when there was a knock on the door. On opening it I was greeted by a short, fat, jolly American who said "Hi sister, we're the soldiers assigned to stay with you." I showed them to their bedroom where they deposited their kit, before going back to Victoria Park for their meal.'

The two men in question were Sergeant Martin McCarthy from St Louis and Ray Haylett from Albuquerque, where he had been the manager of the cinema before going into the Army. He went over to

34 Another painting by Roger Lane, 'Hope and Glory,' showing that the harvesting had to go on. (Reproduced with the permission of Roger Lane).

France with the invasion forces, but was repatriated shortly afterwards as his only child was very ill with polio. His wife sent Molly a silver bracelet made by the Navajo Indians, who, Ray had told her, would enter their home uninvited and join them for meals.

Sergeant McCarthy wrote to Molly from France and notes: 'As I write this I have one of his cards in front of me. My mother kept in touch with him and his wife until his death but continued to write to his wife. My mother died in 1971 and I then kept in touch with his wife until her death two years ago at the age of 95. I visited her and her four children and many grand and great grandchildren on the occasion of her 85th birthday. I still keep in touch with her youngest daughter and feel very much a part of their family.'

In many instances, these young American servicemen kept in touch with their friends in England who had kindly given them room and board at such a difficult time in their lives, and, as in the case of Molly Owen and Sergeant McCarthy, relationships have continued to exist through subsequent generations.

Chapter 3

Getting to Know You

Having settled into their respective camps, bases, and other forms of accommodation, it was inevitable that the Americans would begin to venture beyond the confines of their new homes. This might have been for a variety of reasons and, although they would normally still be wearing uniform while in public, perhaps it offered a chance to stop being soldiers for a while, to forget their enforced military life. It was an opportunity to experience the culture, towns and countryside of a land that many considered their ancestral homeland, and to meet local people, other than those with whom they might be living or working.

As the Americans began to familiarise themselves with Britain and its people, likewise the British were coming to know them. So did the GIs live up to Britain's pre-conceived ideas about them? Were the 'Yanks' really the brash, arrogant, extroverts that people had expected, or did they also have a gentler, more caring and generous nature as well? And what about the Americans? Were the 'Brits' as stuffy as they had been led to believe, or did they have a warmer side to their character?

Friends of the Family

Bob Powell, nicknamed 'Punchy', who earlier told of his experience of living with the Edwards family in Bushey, got to know several other families during his time in England serving with the 8th Air Force. The first of these were the Brookes family in Eaton Constantine, near Shrewsbury in Shropshire, who left a lasting impression on him.

A few days after arriving in Liverpool in April 1943 aboard the *Avant Pasteur* (a French liner converted to troop carrier), he was assigned to an RTU (Replacement Training Unit) at Atcham, near Shrewsbury, in order to obtain additional combat flight training in P-47 Thunderbolts, the aircraft he would eventually fly in combat. As a newly commissioned 2nd lieutenant he was hoping to add a few extra hours in Thunderbolts to the 50 he had already clocked up at flying school in the United States. No such luck, because, when they arrived at Atcham, there weren't enough P-47s available to keep everyone busy. Instead, they were allowed to practise on any other planes on the airfield, which included some 'old war-weary' Battle of Britain Spitfires, which he thinks were Mark IVs; and a few American L-4 Piper Cubs. Never having flown either of these aircraft before, he jumped at the opportunity to

35 Phil Natale, who was one of six brothers in uniform during the Second World War. He was one of the many Yanks that Brenda Gower met at dances around Andover. On the back of the photo he had written: 'to a very sweet girl from your sincere friend.' (Photo: courtesy of Brenda Gower)

get some flying time in both, and it was while he was doing this that he encountered the Brookes family for the first time.

'One day Johnny Woods and I took one of the Cubs out to look over the beautiful countryside at low level,' he recalls, 'to get the lay of the land. Just west of Atcham we spotted two girls on horseback and circled them at about 500 feet until they returned to their village home in Eaton Constantine. When they arrived at their home it appeared to be the biggest house in the village. They dismounted and turned their horses over to two young men, whom we later learned were Italian prisoners-of-war captured in Africa (near Tobruk, I think) and assigned to the family to help with the farm. Anyway, good fighter pilots are always aggressive, so as I circled around the village at about 300 feet, Johnny took a pencil and piece of paper out of his flight suit pocket and wrote a note on it that went something like this, "We'll be over to see you soon." Johnny wrapped the note around the pencil and took a rubber band from around the ankle of his flight suit and secured it. I then flew the plane down between the Dutch Barn and their big house and he threw it out the window of the Cub into their yard. By this time the whole village was out to see what was happening. One of the girls picked up the note, read it and waved, and of course, we took this for a "Yes", wagged our wings and headed back to Atcham, noting the winding roads leading back to our base for future use.'

A few days later, when they weren't doing any flying, Bob Powell and Johnny Woods decided to pay the girls a visit. Getting on their bikes – 'everyone was assigned a bike', he notes – they made their way to the village of Eaton Constantine, which at the time he recalls comprised about 15-20 families. Arriving at the largest house, which was identified by a small sign on the wall reading 'Eaton House', they discovered a tall lady standing just inside the gate.

In his very best southern manner Bob said, 'Good morning, Ma'am!' and she acknowledged the greeting. Then, while circling his fingers over his head he explained, 'We are the pilots who were over here the other day'. The woman responded with, 'Oh, yes, and I suppose you came to meet our daughters?' 'Yes, Ma'am,' replied Bob, 'I suppose we did.'

The lady, Mrs Gladys Brookes, invited them into the house and in the living room introduced them to her husband, William Brookes. They sat and talked for almost an hour, but there was no sign of the girls. 'We talked about what we thought of England,' says Bob, 'about the airfield at Atcham, about the town of Shrewsbury, and about where in America we came from – interesting conversation, but still no girls.'

Eventually, Mrs Brookes offered them some tea and went into her kitchen to prepare it, while the two pilots continued talking to Mr Brookes. When the lady returned she was at last accompanied by her two daughters, Kay and Mary, who were helping her with the tea service. The conversation continued for almost another hour, until Bob, not wanting to overstay their welcome, remarked that they should be getting back to Atcham.

Mr Brookes asked them by which route they had come to the village and, when told, he explained that there was a shorter way and started to give them directions. One of the girls interrupted him to say, 'Papa, we will get on our bikes and show them the way'.

'And that is when we got acquainted', notes Bob. Riding back towards Atcham, they stopped and sat down together on the side of the road, talked and got to know each other. They also arranged to revisit them at an early date.

'This was our first acquaintance with the English girls and we had "lucked-out" by meeting the daughters of a gentleman farmer, who was not only the village leader but owned and trained race horses as well. My mother had always told me, "It is better to be lucky than good looking" and we had just enjoyed being lucky.'

36   Eaton Constantine from the air as Bob Powell first saw it in 1943, showing Eaton House in the upper right, home of the Brookes family. (Photo: courtesy of Bob Powell)

During the following months, while training at Atcham, the pilots forged close friendships with the whole of the Brookes family, as Bob goes on to explain. 'When we would arrive on our bikes and enter the gates to their home we were often greeted by the two Italian prisoners-of-war, Troise and Herman, with a snappy Fascist salute. Mr Brookes taught us how to play darts and we often played with him. Since neither Johnny nor I smoked, we brought him American cigarettes which he enjoyed and we sort of became "adopted sons" to the parents. The girls, although a few years younger than Johnny and me, were not only quite attractive but a lot of fun. We would sometimes ride the horses and have picnics together on the Wrekin, a legendary hill near the village. Mr Brookes also loaned me his car one night to take the girls to a dance we were having at the base officers' club. On at least one occasion the girls invited us to accompany them to a dance in a nearby village – Leighton, about two and a half miles from Eaton.'

Unfortunately, a few weeks later Johnny Woods was killed in a flying accident, when the wing of his Spitfire clipped a tree, causing it to crash into the ground while they were out simulating a strafing attack. After Johnny's death Bob Powell invited two other pilots from Atcham to visit the Brookes family with him, Charley Reed and Fred Windemere. They also enjoyed the hospitality of this friendly English family, particularly Charley, who had been a cavalryman in the US Army before becoming an aviation cadet. Charley really knew about horses, so Mr Brookes took to him straight away, and even let him ride one of his horses in a race, in which Bob Powell believes he came third.

'In August, however,' Bob concludes, 'they started assigning us to one of the four American fighter groups then stationed in East Anglia. I was assigned to the 352nd stationed at Bodney, just south of Norwich. That more or less ended our relationship with the family except that on one occasion when I was slow-timing a new engine in my P-47 at Bodney I got permission to fly back and had a final visit with the

37   P-47 Thunderbolt and P-51 Mustang, two American fighter aircraft employed on British airbases during the Second World War. (Photo: Author)

38 George Rarey's cartoon entitled 'Our New Home', which gives a good idea of what the Americans thought of the weather at Headcorn in Kent. (Illustration: courtesy of Linda Rarey and the EAA Museum)

Brookes family – until 2003, but that is another story – and a much more fascinating one.'

In 1944 Beryl Glenister was in the Land Army and stationed at Woodgreen near Fordingbridge on the edge of the New Forest. The Yanks would send a truck to pick up anyone who would like to attend their dances at Dinton near Salisbury. At one of these dances Beryl met a master sergeant called Albert Hoffer, looking very unhappy. He was married, missing his wife, and about to enjoy seven days' leave with nowhere to go. Beryl told him that her parents kept an open house for anyone in uniform if he would like to stay in Christchurch. He accepted and, on her next convenient weekend off, she took him home. From

39 Beryl Glenister with Albert Hoffer (far left) and other friends at Christchurch Quay. (Photo: courtesy of Beryl Glenister)

that visit Albert became part of the family and even celebrated the end of the war with them.

On returning home to Sacramento Albert promised to write and was true to his word. Forty-two years later, Albert and his wife Dagny re-visited his wartime family and Beryl and her husband accompanied them back to Dinton, where they danced in the field where the Nissen huts, in which they had first met, once stood. After that they went into the village shop where the owner was still the same lady as all those years before. Although Albert now had grey hair, when he entered the shop and spoke she remembered him immediately saying, 'You were the master sergeant who used to get us for your film shows'.

Sheilah Skingley, who was 17, had an American boyfriend called Clem Dwyer, who was stationed at Wethersfield in Essex. Her sister Muriel Williamson recalls him being 'a gentleman'. Whenever he visited their house in Rothesay Avenue, Chelmsford, he would bring the customary gift of food, conscious of the strict rationing placed on the British. Clem wanted to marry Sheilah, but because he was a staunch Catholic, her mother said 'No'. So instead, he remained friends with her and the rest of the family and, after leaving to go back to America, he began writing to them.

Clem's letters from that time are a fine contemporary record and indication of his feelings towards his relationship with the Skingley family, and make us realise how important these

40   After many happy visits to the Skingley family in Essex, Clem kept in touch by letter on his return to America at the end of 1943. (Photo: courtesy of Muriel Williamson)

41   Clem pictured in Maldon, Essex in 1943 with his 'Dear Mother Skingley', and The Corporal. (Photo: courtesy of Muriel Williamson)

wartime associations were, even after these young men had gone home. Sadly, we know very little about Clem, other than that he was an officer and, from photographs, possibly came from the Boston area. His photos alone prove him to be full of character and fun. The first quote is taken from a letter penned on New Year's Eve, 1943, addressed to 'Dear Mother Skingley', in which he writes:

> I really don't know how I can ever thank you for the hospitality you showed me. I only hope that I can get back that way again sometime. I haven't the slightest idea where I'll go from here but first I have got to go through this course. And it is a rather rough place to be. I could almost compare it to the 'glass house'. We have to double time everywhere we go. We have to work military training in with our academic courses. They add up to about 16 or 18 hours a day. We have three hours on Sunday afternoon off – (that means we can leave the barracks but not the fort). Today we happened to be lucky, they made New Year's Day a holiday – all day.
>
> My only regret is that I was only able to get home for one day when I arrived from overseas. I was sent directly here. If I should pass I may get a 10-day leave – I hope.
>
> A funny thing happened when I got here. I found out that my brother, Leo, had arrived in England about two days after I left. Isn't that rotten luck?
>
> I hope you had a nice Christmas. I imagine you did since the 'Corporal' was supposed to be home then, wasn't he?

The final sentence, regarding the Corporal refers to Muriel's father, who was serving in the Army Fire Service. In the next quote, dated 1 April 1944, just over a month before D-Day, where he refers to 'your Monday after Sunday dish', he is describing 'Bubble & Squeak'.

> How has everything been going at the little institution attached to the 'Cherry Tree', or should I say to which the 'Cherry Tree' is attached. There must have been something in the English beer. I could drink and it wasn't too bad, but I have tried to drink the beer here but I can't take it. Guess I'm just not a drinker – milk, yes, but nothing stronger.
>
> I've been to Washington a few times but I've never run across anything to eat that I like as much as your 'Monday after Sunday dish'. That sure used to be good. I don't think that could ever be duplicated here.
>
> To get away from the subject of food – even though it is my favorite one – I imagine by the time you get this I will have probably left this place for some unknown destination. I just hope it's the right way.

The *Cherry Tree* was a pub in Chelmsford, which has since closed. The envelope to this letter, which was the last they ever received from Clem, indicates that he was at Fort Belvoir, Virginia. We have no idea of where he went from there, or indeed, as Muriel Williamson poignantly states, 'I can only imagine what might have happened to him'. But whatever did happen to Clem, his letters are testimony to the impression that one British family made on him.

A WARM WELCOME TO ALL

Nellie Middleton, the mother of Jennifer Mason, had many friends and acquaintances in the United States, as a result of being a member of the Church of Jesus Christ of Latter Day Saints whose headquarters were in Salt Lake City, Utah.

As American soldiers began to pour into Cheltenham, she thought them quite likely to include young members of the church who might appreciate contact with a friendly English face. As well as camps at places like Pittville Park and Prestbury Park racecourse, many hotels in the town were being used to accommodate the troops, including *The Queens Hotel*, and Nan (as Mrs Middleton was known) happened to know the officer in charge. Having told the man her aim, he suggested putting up a notice in the foyer of the hotel. The notice included a small picture of the Salt Lake Temple painted by her sister, that any church member would instantly recognise, and the promise that any one interested was welcome to call at their house.

'These were years of blackout,' states Jennifer, 'so when a knock came at the door on a dark November evening in 1943 and an American voice introduced himself as Ray J. Hermansen, she couldn't see the figure, but just held out her hand and invited him in! So Ray was the first of dozens of servicemen who joined us around the fireside. Many others came during the coming months. Some we only saw once, and others became life-long friends.'

Jennifer recalls how many of these young men were extremely homesick and frightened of what lay ahead. Their lives were regimented but they had hours of nothing to do in a strange country, where travel was limited and friendly faces rare. One night in December 1944 she recalls how Marty Cox, who had visited the house several times, brought another soldier with him from the 106th Infantry Division, on the eve of their deployment to the front. The young man beautifully sang Mallotte's *The Lord's Prayer* unaccompanied, and many tears were shed in the house that night. The boy was barely 18, and later Marty Cox told the family that he had been killed shortly afterwards at the Battle of the Bulge.

Many of these young men had enlisted straight from college and Jennifer remembers how her mother would comfort them. 'The boys,' she says, 'seemed to find in our home, a haven in a difficult period in their lives. An evening with us, having a sing-song with the piano, or playing childish games with me, seemed to alleviate their stress.'

Nan's house was open to many, not merely the Americans, and among those who had come to stay was her friend Doris Hanman, at the time recovering from a serious illness. One GI, Bill Overley from Salt Lake City, would accompany Doris on cycle rides. She would sit on her 'old sit-up-and-beg bike', as Jennifer describes it, while Bill would arrive on a camp bike painted regulation khaki, and talk continually of his girlfriend Adell, whom he hoped to marry one day.

'My mother died many years ago,' Jennifer concludes, 'but she had a great influence for good on some of the American servicemen and we have treasured their friendships throughout the years.'

At Axminster in Devon, a
US military hospital was built in
preparation for the evacuation of
battle casualties from Normandy.
This was one of several hospitals
built in the area, which also
included the larger hospital at
Musgrove in Taunton, still in use
today. The complex at Axminster
was constructed mostly of wood,
with the personnel of 4th Platoon,
3rd Special Service Unit housed
in tents. Sheila Pitman's father,
Reginald Perham, worked there
as a storeman and would bring
several Americans home. One,
who was called Curtis, celebrated
his 21st birthday with them, so
Sheila's mother Marjorie baked
a cake for the occasion. Curtis
would take some of the local
children swimming in the nearby
river and must have been very
strong because Sheila remembers

42   Bill Overley, one of the Americans from
Salt Lake City who would visit the home
of Nan Middleton in Cheltenham. This
photograph was sent from France. (Photo:
courtesy of Jennifer Mason)

him carrying her three brothers at the same time: one under each arm,
and the third on his shoulders.

One of Sheila's strangest memories concerns Bob Land, who was in
charge of the medical stores, and had a daughter back home about the
same age as her youngest brother. Sheila's mother kindly made a dress
for him to send home, using her brother as the model, in order for him
to have an idea of what the dress would look like on his daughter.

Sheila will never forget the Americans who befriended her family
that summer of 1944, not only because her cousin married one, but
because, after the war, the huts were knocked down and the wards
converted into council flats, one of which her family moved into in
1948.

Many black soldiers were also readily welcomed into British homes.
During the early part of the war Betty Currah recalls that internationally
known black singer, John Payne, was invited to escape the Blitz on
London and stay at the home of Lady Cook at her home in Talland
near Looe in Cornwall. Betty was 14, and was introduced to him at
a local concert, which resulted in him giving her singing lessons. He
had already formed a local concert party giving concerts around south-
east Cornwall for the war effort. Then in 1943, American troops were
stationed in the area around Looe and Liskeard, among them a company
of black soldiers who were billeted at Doublebois House. On learning of
this John Payne quickly made contact with them and eventually formed
a choir, singing spirituals. Some of these soldiers began to visit Betty's
parents at their home in Looe. A couple of them, Sergeant Bradshaw
and Private John Layman, came to stay with them during their leave

time, forming a close friendship. They often brought tins of fruit and Camel cigarettes for her father, as well as a US Army torch she recalls, which her father treasured until his death.

'In mid-1944 they suddenly stopped coming,' writes Betty. 'We later realized they had been part of the invasion force. Some time after the war my parents had a letter from Sergeant Bradshaw conveying his appreciation for their kindness and hospitality. At that time there was a lot of prejudice and it was frowned on by some people, to invite black men into your home.'

Lorna Rundle first met black Americans when they visited the village of Mount Hawke in Cornwall, where she lived with her mother and father, Mr and Mrs Mewton, who ran a butcher's shop. The soldiers were camped in fields opposite St Agnes railway station, and their first real introduction to Cornish society was when a group of them gave a sacred concert in the chapel.

'Different families took them home for tea,' she recalls, 'but they all eventually ended up coming to our house. Most Sunday evenings they would come to our home, where they would sing for my father. Then they would all get in my father's van and go for a couple of beers. While they were gone, my mother and her friend would make pork pies, so that they could have supper before returning to St Agnes camp.'

Lorna also tells of how the other villagers would congregate outside the house and lean on the wall, trying to hear the soldiers singing. 'Shame they wouldn't invite them into their own homes,' she points out, emphasising again the evident racism in rural Britain at the time: or was it simply ignorance?

Brian Bawden was 13 in 1944, living at Threemilestone near Truro in Cornwall, when hundreds of American soldiers settled in the area for several months before taking part in the invasion. They lived in a tented camp, which became a restricted area. Because Brian lived within this restricted area, he had to walk two miles each day to catch the school bus, at the nearest stop that was outside it. His mother kept the local Post Office and he sometimes took mail on his bike to a spot outside the area to be collected by the post van, as even Post Office vehicles were not allowed within the restricted zone.

43   Personnel of the 3rd Special Service Unit outside the American Army hospital at Axminster in Devon, built to receive the wounded following D-Day. Curtis, on the right, celebrated his 21st birthday at the camp, for which Sheila Pitman's mother baked him a cake. (Photo: courtesy of Sheila Pitman)

'Both black and white American soldiers were stationed here,' he recalls. 'They were all very friendly to the local people, coming regularly into our homes. It was wonderful for me to get plenty of sweets, tinned fruit and tinned soup, which the Americans very generously gave us. One white American became very friendly with a girl who worked for my mother in her Post Office stores, and would probably have married her had he not been killed crossing the Rhine. Another white soldier, who regularly came into my home, came to stay with us later for a week while on leave from Europe.'

One black soldier, who regularly came to their house, admitted to not wanting to fight, and would sometimes stay well after the expiry time on his pass. On leaving, although he would say, 'I'll be back', it was often a considerable time before he did return, as he was restricted to

44   Bob Land (right), who had a daughter back in the States about the same age as Sheila Pitman's younger brother. Her mother made a dress for his daughter, using her son as the fitting model. (Photo: courtesy of Sheila Pitman)

camp as a punishment. Brian also recalls a group of black soldiers taking a service at the Methodist church, when they sang several negro spirituals.

'I remember seeing a game of baseball for the first time,' he notes, 'played by White American soldiers in a local field. Both white and black soldiers played various card games with us in our homes. We were taught for example how to play 500 rummy. I was introduced to the game of draughts by an English lieutenant who was attached to the American Army, and who lived in a tent right outside my home. I learnt more of the skill of the game from white American soldiers. This was the beginning of a lifelong interest for me. Since then I have played draughts for Cornwall, and for England, against Ireland, Scotland and Wales.'

Lois Taylor was 13 years old on Christmas Day 1944. Her father had died in 1942 and she was having Christmas tea with her mother and sisters, Cynthia who was 15 and Rita six years old. She lived in Whitchurch, Hampshire, and there was a large army camp at Barton Stacey about three miles away. She looked out of the window and saw two Americans walking along the road and back again, and begged her mother to send Rita out and invite them to share their tea.

Rita brought the two GIs into the front room (only used at Christmas). They were most polite, their names being Charles Bachus and James

45 Tea time
at the NAAFI
truck for 303rd
ground personnel
at Molesworth.
(Photo: courtesy
of Mark Forlow)

46 The group of black soldiers who regularly visited the home of Mr and Mrs Mewton in Mount Hawke, Cornwall, who are also seen in the picture. (Photo: courtesy of Lorna Rundle)

Henry Moore. Her father had been teetotal and non-smoking, but her mother had managed to buy a bottle of sherry from somewhere. So Lois found it very exciting to speak to them and smell Camel cigarettes and they returned several times, bringing Olin Wiggins from Florida, Roy Brown from Texas, and Ed Humphries from New York. They used to drop in on the way back from the pub, although drink was never brought into the house. Lois would make the men cocoa, and cheese and tomato sandwiches, before they went back to camp. Also at weekends they came for Sunday lunch and particularly liked her mother's apple pie, bringing the children sweets in return.

Lois doesn't know what units these men served with, only that they were infantrymen and says, 'There were of course many convoys passing my house, and tanks, which I found very exciting. The children used to wave to every convoy and the soldiers would throw out packets of chewing gum and sweets. I was very upset that wives of soldiers serving with the Eighth and Fourteenth Armies, and one a POW, all slept with Americans. The nicest and to me the most devoted of wives walked out with an American, and being 13 it was something I did not understand.'

By 1942 there was a well-established YMCA canteen in Thrapston which was staffed by local volunteers and it was used by British and American service-men and women. Members of Monica Mercer's family were regular helpers at the canteen, so there were many opportunities to chat to service personnel of all nationalities. It was through this contact that her mother, on many occasions, invited some of the men or women of the forces

47 Tommy, who would have married the girl in the Post Office, had he not been killed crossing the Rhine. (Photo: courtesy of Brian Bawden)

to their home, for a meal and a chat. 'During the years 1943-1945,' states Monica, 'we had three fairly regular American visitors from Molesworth Airbase who spent some of their off-duty time with us and became part of the family. They did appreciate the chance to relax and get away from the pressures they were under and have contact with an English family. I clearly remember they called my father "Pop" and my mother "Mom". One was from Texas, one from Ohio and the third from Massachusetts. They were always pleasant company and eventually their families back home began to correspond with my mother, and send us food parcels. At Christmas 1944, one of the three spent the Christmas holiday with us (for three days I think) and I can remember how much we all enjoyed eating tinned peaches and a most wonderful fruit cake on Christmas Day, which had been sent by his family. Sheer luxury to us, as our food was rationed. On looking back, I often wonder how my mother was able to feed extra people in those days of wartime restrictions and food shortages.'

A GENEROUS NATURE

Time and time again we learn about the generosity of the wartime Yanks towards their British cousins. To some extent this was an attempt to be accepted, but by the sheer volume of evidence it is obvious that generosity was a sincere characteristic of Americans at the time.

The parents of Margaret Sproit, Mr and Mrs Anderson, were always willing to welcome Americans into their home at Newbury Park in Essex, one of whom proved to be particularly generous, although as it transpired, the opportunity and means to do so were readily at hand.

There was an American base at Hainault down a country lane near their home and their relationship with the American in question began when Margaret and a friend were cycling down this lane and were spoken to by a couple of GIs. 'With no other intention in mind,' recalls Margaret, 'other than to say "hello" we stopped, told them where the local shops were, and the bigger town of Ilford.' The Americans wanted to know where they could catch the bus, and in the end the two young ladies walked them to the nearest bus stop.

One of the GIs, who Margaret recalls being very 'chatty', was called Percy O'Mahlen, who hailed from Los Angeles. He appeared to be rather homesick and, as she lived down a road opposite their lane, Margaret gave Percy her address. The following afternoon there was a knock at the door and there stood Percy asking if he could pay the family a visit. It transpired that Percy was in charge of the PX club, and boasted that if they wanted anything, they only had to ask!

After that Percy became a regular caller at their home, and he and Mr Anderson got on 'like a house on fire'. He had a younger brother called Duane, about to join the Army himself, and Margaret thinks that, back home in the States, the two boys only had their mother. 'Percy used to bring so many things for us,' she explains, 'we never asked, but he would insist because we had made him feel welcome. He brought my father officers' trousers made from beautiful material, as well as tins of corned beef, large tins of fruit, chocolate, socks, etc. We eventually met Duane, who was a quieter version of Percy, also well mannered and homesick.'

Sadly, when the boys went overseas, they lost contact with them and didn't know their fate. Then in 1946 they received a letter from Percy, with photos of both him and Duane enjoying themselves in Long Beach, California – they'd both made it safely home to their mother.

There was also a certain amount of give and take between the two camps. For instance, at Tibenham in Norfolk, Dorothy Knapp's father would pickle onions and red cabbage, which one American absolutely adored, and would swap for fresh meat. She recalls that around 30 minutes after watching supply planes coming into land, their American friend would turn up at the house with a haversack on his back, with blood oozing out of the bottom. No questions asked!

On Christmas Eve 1943, Cyril Guscott found himself in the Princess Elizabeth Orthopaedic

48   The American who came to stay. After going to France on D-Day, this American soldier returned to Brian Bawden's home in Cornwall, when he had leave. (Photo: courtesy of Brian Bawden)

Hospital in Barrack Road, Exeter, near Topsham Barracks. The Americans moved in at about the same time and began to visit the patients, bringing the usual bag of goodies that hadn't been seen since before the war. One young man who visited frequently from the barracks was Christy Briest, and he and Cyril soon became great friends. Cyril was 23 years old, and serving as a lieutenant in the Devonshire Regiment. He had been in various hospitals since an operation in May 1943 to remove his appendix in the military hospital at Colchester, where he was serving. A spinal anaesthetic had been used, following which he had developed a tubercular lesion at the site of the injection. So by the time the Americans, and Christy in particular, arrived, he was feeling pretty low.

49   Percy O'Mahlen, who was in charge of the PX at the American camp at Hainault. He would thank the Anderson family for their friendship by bringing them gifts, such as tins of corned beef and fruit. (Photo: courtesy of Margaret Sproit)

> My wife and I were very young and, having married in wartime in 1942, had pretty literally nothing. His friendship meant a lot to us. After you had been ill for six months your pay stopped and I had to wait for a discharge before I could claim a pension. We never forgot him and many others. After they left for Normandy we never heard of any of them again.

Another story of generosity of a different sort is related by Iris Thomas, whose father worked as a groom at Boddington Manor near Cheltenham, where her family lived on the estate in a tied cottage. Early in the war the manor house itself and Boddington House Farm were taken over by the British military, and later the Americans moved in.

The cottage in which Iris lived was between the manor house and the farm, so if she was playing in the garden when soldiers passed on their way to meals at the manor, they would stop to talk or throw candy over the hedge. Two Yanks in particular, called Eddie and Lamb, became especially friendly with her whole family.

Occasionally there would be a whist drive and dance held at the school in Staverton, the next village, which the Americans loved to attend. On one occasion, just before her brother's fifth birthday, all her family went along and met up with Eddie and Lamb at the dance afterwards. At the dance there was a raffle and the first prize was a decorated iced cake. Eddie and Lamb decided to try to win the cake for her brother's birthday, spending a lot of money on raffle tickets. They also persuaded some of their friends to chip in as well, to buy up

50 An ambulance with its crew and equipment at Wendling in Norfolk. (Photo: courtesy of www. b24.net)

as many tickets as possible. At the end of the evening the raffle was drawn and, luckily, one of the Americans had the winning ticket. It was arranged that everyone who had helped to win the cake would call round the next day to share it.

Iris woke early the next day full of excitement, but their friends didn't show up. The family was shocked to learn that during the night the Americans had been moved out suddenly and nobody heard a thing. So they had no option but to eat the cake on their own. Weeks later they heard through a girl in the village, who was courting one of the GIs, that her boyfriend along with many others in his unit had been killed.

Bryan White lived in Underhill on Portland throughout the war where he recalls the Invasion Holding Car Park on Weymouth Road. He had a Sunday paper-round and, after finishing it, would take papers out for the Americans at the car park, about two miles away. He didn't mind the trip because most of the GIs paid with £1 notes, rarely asking for change.

One day, after delivering his papers, he was wandering back down the line of parked vehicles when he saw a group of soldiers tossing coins into a tin, from behind a line that had been grooved into the ground. Bryan leant against a lorry and watched as each man in turn would approach the line and throw coins of all denominations at the tin. Those that went in were accompanied by a chorus of cheers, while those that didn't were greeted with ribald remarks. Bryan watched with amazement having never seen so much money in his life, yet here were the Yanks just throwing it around. He was even more amazed, when, tired of the game, one of the soldiers picked up all the money that had fallen short, placed it inside the tin, approached him and tipped the lot into the bag in which he carried his newspapers. 'I never knew how much was in the paper bag,' says Bryan, 'I only know it was heavy. I hurried straight home and gave it to my parents, before anybody could take it from me.'

Pat Robinson remembers very clearly her first meeting with Jimmy Robbins, her knight in shining armour. One evening, after her mother had taken her into Cheltenham to see some friends, they boarded the wrong train home. They should have been going to Stroud but were heading in the wrong direction, and realising their mistake got off the train at the first available stop: a place called Andoversford. Trains from here back to Cheltenham were few and far between, so they eventually caught one to Gloucester, which at least took them in the right direction. At Gloucester, they discovered that a mail train ran to Stroud, due in around midnight.

The couple hadn't eaten since lunchtime, so when they crossed the bridge to the opposite platform and saw a busy canteen, their hearts sank after reading the notice that stated 'Forces Only'. Bitterly disappointed, they were about to turn away when a voice behind them asked if they wanted a cup of tea.

The voice belonged to a GI who promptly found them a seat, before buying them both tea and sandwiches. 'He refused to let us pay him,' says Pat, 'and stayed and talked to us, asking where we were going. When we said "Stroud" he said, "You'd better stick with me or you'll never get on. I know the mail train and it's always crowded." He told us his name was Jimmy Robbins and that he was stationed with the 188th General Hospital Unit on the outskirts of Cirencester.'

Jimmy was quite short and stocky which Pat explains proved very useful, because when the train finally arrived, he went straight into action, blocking the doorway to make sure that nobody else could board the train before them! He was quite right, the train was heaving and they would never have managed without his help. They stood in a crowded corridor but arrived safely at Stroud, by which time they had given Jimmy directions to their house, which was about a mile from the station, inviting him to visit them. Luckily for Pat, her father was a clerk at Stroud GWR station and, having contacted him earlier by phone, he was there to meet them. Jimmy himself stayed on the train until Kemble, from where he had to walk back to his unit, as, although there was a branch line to Cirencester, there were no connecting trains so late at night.

Jimmy visited the family on many occasions and was always made very welcome. In return for their hospitality, he always arrived with a bag of goodies for the family, which was always placed on the same chair. Pat was always bursting to know what was inside the bag, but she would never look until Jimmy asked her to do so.

Pat's parents celebrated both their daughter's 17th birthday and VE Day in May 1945 with a single celebration at Rodborough church hall. They were not well off, and previous birthday parties had always been held in their house, so she knew this was a very special occasion. A pianist provided music, and there was even some modest outside catering. Jimmy attended with one of his army friends and Pat was surprised to discover that her stocky knight in armour was an excellent dancer. He even brought her a birthday present, a pretty little necklace that she still treasures.

Another American hero came to the rescue of Lomond Handley's brother Adrian, when he and his mother were forced into a Bournemouth air-raid shelter during an air raid. The little boy was caught short and wanted to use his potty, which was still at their flat. His mother took him by the hand and was about to lead him back out of the shelter when an American soldier said, 'Hey, where do you think you're going, honey?' With some embarrassment, the boy's mother explained the situation, at which the GI removed his helmet, and gave it to Adrian to use as a potty. The child went happily into a corner to relieve himself, after which the soldier laughed, emptied the helmet out of the shelter, and then put it back on his head.

51 Jimmy Robbins, a knight in shining armour, who served with the 188th General Hospital Unit on the outskirts of Cirencester. (Photo: courtesy of Pat Robinson)

In Buckinghamshire, Mrs A. Highley recalls that American troops were stationed at Wycombe Abbey. Being in her teens she worked at a day nursery, while during the evenings she helped out at the British Army canteen, used by soldiers stationed at nearby Hazlemere.

At the canteen the ladies served tea, accompanied by biscuits or cakes kindly donated by local people and businesses. There was also a box of loose cigarettes on a table, likewise donated so that the soldiers could have a smoke during the evening. On one occasion the canteen was full of soldiers in muddy uniforms, having just finished military manoeuvres. The door opened and in walked four immaculate Americans, asking if they could have a coffee? The serving ladies explained that they only offered tea, which they gratefully accepted.

Having recently arrived in England the men were having a look around. Shaking hands with the British soldiers, they asked about the box of cigarettes, to be informed that every soldier was entitled to 'one only' each evening. As the occasion progressed, one of the Americans disappeared, only to return again later clutching cartons of cigarettes, giving every man present a full pack each.

The Americans attended the canteen regularly after that, always bringing sweets or cigarettes and, after learning that Mrs Highley worked at a nursery, they soon turned up there as well in their Jeep, bringing boxes of sweets, biscuits and dried bananas, that she describes as looking like 'squares of grey rubber'.

Chapter 4

Working Together

Some of the strongest relationships that people experience during the course of their lives are with the people they work with. These working relationships might span decades, and are often as intimate, trusting and close as those shared with family and friends. After all, in the normal working week, most people spend more time with their colleagues than they do with anybody else, including their husbands or wives. In Britain during the Second World War, an unusual and unique set of circumstances often threw people together for short and memorable periods of activity. As well as those employed by the armed forces, much of the nation's adult population did some type of war work. Many people did jobs that were completely new to them and which they were unlikely to do again in the future.

As American camps became established all over Britain, many opportunities for employment were on offer for both men and women. Many people worked alongside their trans-Atlantic allies; some worked directly under their control, both in a civil or military capacity; and others used the situation to make a little extra money on the side, offering a wide range of services to willing GIs.

Side by Side

In the 1940s, the vast majority of children left school to begin their working lives when they were 14 years old. Frank Kidwell started work on the railway at Barnstaple Junction in north Devon on 20 August 1942, aged 14 years and four months. He was employed as a number taker, recording the movement of all goods vehicles in and out of the many goods sidings that existed there at the time.

Shortly before his employment started, the Americans had arrived and set up their RTO (Rail Transportation Office) outside what

52 Working together at the highest level. Colonel Kermit Stevens with the King, Queen and Princess Elizabeth, during a visit to Molesworth on 6 July 1944. (Photo: courtesy of 303rd Bomb Group Association)

53   Royal walkabout: doing what she now does best, Princess Elizabeth meets US troops, accompanied by Colonel Stevens, during the royal visit to Molesworth on 6 July 1944. (Photo: courtesy of 303rd Bomb Group Association)

is the present booking hall at Barnstaple Junction. Frank soon discovered that a certain Corporal James G. Owens was doing a parallel task on rail goods traffic for the US Army. 'We soon struck up a friendship,' explains Frank, 'he had digs local to the station.'

Frank's mother, on hearing of Corporal Owens, invited him to Sunday lunch and, as with so many other accounts, one Sunday lunch turned into many. Frank notes that his new friend liked to relax in a home environment.

James Owens was particularly keen on attending any local 'hops' that were being put on in the area and, as well as patronising the dance halls of Barnstaple, such as they were, he would travel to places like Umberleigh and Braunton.

'To help him get to these dances,' continues Frank, 'on occasion I would duplicate parts of my work, which were related to US traffic. I would leave this on his desk, situated in the half-round, galvanised hut that acted as the RTO, ready for him to copy into his own records the following morning. On occasion his CO would catch me doing this, and sometimes a cigar was sent home for my dad and I had gum.'

With the D-Day disappearance of the Yanks, silence reigned for a while, but then the correspondence started and the following extracts from some of Owens' letters give a short record of his return to civilian life and his own recollections of his working colleagues in Devon.

Extract from a letter dated 19 December 1947, sent from Allentown, Pennsylvania:

> Had quite a summer here. Got back home the latter part of April and just loafed and loafed until September when school opened. Sure a lazy man's way of living, but I hadn't had a holiday since I went into the service, and as soon as I got out I went to work, so the few months that I rested was well deserved, for I sure don't have much time to play now.
>
> How do you like shunting? If I remember, that was rather a dangerous job while I was at the RTO. What happened to all the others that were there? Is Syd still working? How about the chap that lives right below Mrs Chugg, where I used to stay, can't think of his name right now. Then there was another fellow who worked in the office directly over from where the RTO was, he lived up near to Syd.

A letter extract dated 30 November 1950, sent from Ithaca, New York:

54 Lord Trenchard, Marshal of the RAF, accompanied by Colonel Stevens, commanding officer of the 303rd Bomb Group, inspects the troops at Molesworth, 4 May 1944. (Photo: courtesy of Mark Forlow)

Often wonder what has become of you and the old gang. The only one I ever hear from, and that is in an indirect way since she writes to my sister, is Grace Chugg, she lived on the terrace and is a member of the family with whom I lived while I was in Barnstaple.

As for me, loads of things have happened. First and most important is the fact that I am now in my last year of school and after six years of hard work, in June of 1952 I will have finished my working in the hospital and will be ready to hang out a shingle and be a licensed medical practitioner in the field of physical medicine. From June the first I will be at a school for mentally defective children in Pennsylvania and after September 15, I will be in New York City at the Hospital for Special Surgery. Am very happy in the work so far and trust to the Good Lord that I may continue as such. Seems a long time to spend in studying, yet as I look back it seems like only yesterday that I started; matter of fact, it seems like only a few days ago that I was RTO at Barnstaple. Often wish I could come back for a visit and I have hopes of seeing my wish come true one of these days.

What has become of all the other buddies there at the station? Suppose they are quite on their way to success in life by now. Incidentally, there are several girls from England living here in Ithaca. They married Americans and I find it interesting to discuss the places I saw while I was there with them. So far I have found no one who lived directly in the places I was stationed, but they are familiar with the land.

James Owens corresponded with Frank for some time and always maintained his wish to return to Barnstaple one day. However, Frank admits that, due to circumstances in both camps, such as address and job changes, they eventually lost touch with each other. 'I wonder if he ever did make it back to Devon?', Frank contemplates.

In the summer of 1940, Mr E.R. Saunders left Dartmouth Grammar School and joined the Great Western Railway (GWR). He found himself based at Brixham on the south Devon coast, not far from his home. In 1942, after being passed unfit for military service, he joined the Railway Home Guard and is today the only surviving member of this section.

The town of Brixham, nestling between Dartmouth and Torquay, was another location to feature in the American invasion plans. It was inevitable, therefore, that, when the Yanks came to the area in 1943 to prepare for the Normandy landings, Mr Saunders would encounter them in his official capacity.

'My first experience of American troops,' he recalls, 'was when I was at Torquay station working on a late turn finishing at midnight.' The troops were constantly training on the coast near Dartmouth and had to be taken to various points by train, often ones that ran through the night. On their return, the empty trains would sometimes wait at Torquay station, which gave the on-duty railway staff the opportunity to look through the empty carriages for anything the GIs might have discarded, such as ration packs, chocolate and sweets.

Many invasion craft sailed for Normandy from the Dartmouth area, and in preparation for this the American Navy constructed a series of slipways, some of which are still in evidence today. At this time Mr Saunders was based at Churston station, which was at the start of the Brixham branch line. He remembers delivering sections of men daily, who were working on the construction of slipways on the river Dart itself, which were needed to pull landing craft out of the river for servicing. He and his railway colleagues all remarked on the friendliness of the US Navy personnel, particularly remembering their invitation to 'help yourselves to any of our food, coffee, and other rations'.

Just before D-Day the American Army opened a refreshment stop on land that belonged to the *Station Inn*, which stood next to Churston

railway station. Here, meals were prepared and served to the troops who were on their way to board the invasion barges moored on the slipways at Brixham and Kingswear. Luckily for Mr Saunders and the other members of the railway staff, the cooks at the canteen would come over to the station and say: 'If you're hungry, come over to us with your plate and help yourself – we have plenty.' Mr Saunders accepted the invitation and for roughly a fortnight enjoyed food that he hadn't tasted in a long while, including various meats, and of course bananas!

After D-Day itself, one of the most ambitious projects he re-members on the Brixham branch line was that a large field hospital had to be transported by rail to Plymouth. It had originally been set up about a mile from Churston station, partly in fields and partly in woods. The hospital was in-

55 Corporal James Owens, who worked in the American RTO (Rail Transportation Office) at Barnstaple, pictured in full kit. This photo was taken at what is now the car park for B&Q, which in 1943 was the embankment leading to Barnstaple Junction Station. (Photo: courtesy of Frank Kidwell)

tended for emergencies but never used. It was conveyed on two special trains, one for passengers and one for freight. No doubt from Plymouth it was destined for France.

Both parents of Pamela Moyse worked for the Americans at a large camp near Southampton, the 14th Major Port US Army Transportation Corps. Her father was exempt from military service in Britain due to his flat feet, so the Americans employed him as a driver for their coaches. He consequently drove their troops all over England. While this was going on her mother worked in the American canteen. The young Pamela, who was about eight or nine, would spend many hours sitting in the rest room waiting for her mother to finish work. There was never a problem with baby-sitters, because while she was there the GIs would keep her company and entertain her. Some would play cards with her, while another man, a black soldier who she recalls had a beautiful voice, would sing to her.

Bryan Huxtable's father was a veteran of the First World War and didn't relish the thought of going through it all again. He was the proprietor of a small building firm, forced to close because all of his male employees had gone into the armed forces. So instead, he found a job with the Devon County Royal Engineers – a branch of the War Department, with their headquarters in Barnstaple High Street. He was taken on as a clerk of works and put in charge of setting up searchlight camps all over north Devon. This involved finding suitable

56   The father of Pamela Moyse worked for the Americans of the 14th Major Port US Army Transportation Corps, while based at a camp near Southampton. Just before the invasion, Tidworth Hill on Salisbury Plain was covered with tanks, Jeeps, trucks and every type of vehicle imaginable. In this picture Alan J. Stewart from Belmont, Massachusetts, a Tidworth-based GI, poses on his Jeep in front of 14th Major Port Headquarters. (Photo: courtesy of Hazel Green)

pieces of land on many local farms and overseeing the construction of the camps.

He was then given the job of overseeing the construction of a large camp at Braunton, to accommodate 30,000 American troops, mainly infantry soldiers sent to train in the sand dunes. America's main ATC (Assault Training Center) was at Woolacombe. Bryan's father arrived on the site about two weeks after a contingent of engineers had already started the work. To his horror he found that they were digging trenches for drains, in soft soil, but without shoring the sides to a suitable depth, which he says should have been between 12 and 14 feet. He immediately complained to the American officer in charge, demanding that the work should stop until the fault had been rectified. The officer proved most unhelpful, and it wasn't until three or four men had been killed in an accident after being buried alive, that any action was taken.

Mr Huxtable's immediate boss was an Irish major by the name of O'Hara, who was known to enjoy a drink. By contrast, the American colonel who was in charge of the camp was something of a disciplinarian, always lecturing his men on the demons of drink. One night, some of the American boys begged the major to try to get the colonel drunk in the camp bar. He succeeded in this aim, and as the couple left the bar later, they both fell into one of the drain trenches, partly filled with muddy water. Delighted onlookers pulled the filthy men out of the ditch and dried them off. Later, Major O'Hara discovered that his pockets had been stuffed with money.

57   Another good example of local people working with the Americans, at the many Red Cross clubs in which local ladies helped out. In this picture, Sally, an American Red Cross Entertainment Officer (left), is pictured in Devizes in September 1945. (Photo: courtesy of Elsie Lewis)

'On another of his inspections,' Bryan relates, 'he had to visit a lookout hut at Saunton Sands, perhaps a couple of miles from the camp. This was to ascertain if there were any repairs needed.' This hut had been set up to aid the target practice of heavy guns. The target itself had been constructed on the beach and the hut was in the beach car park. From here a lookout could observe the target and report back to the gunners by telephone, advising them of their results.

'My father,' notes Bryan, 'arrived during a lull in the firing, so was unaware of what was going on. He was ushered into the hut and told to stay there until he was given permission to leave. After a short while the guns started firing again and two or three shots went safely over the hut. Then, the lookout jumped on my father and dragged him under the stout table that occupied a greater part of the hut, telling him to lie still. With that a shell entered one end of the hut, bounced off the table and disappeared out the other end of the hut to finish somewhere in the sand dunes. The lookout had certainly saved my father's life and needless to say he tore the gunners off a strip or two. And of course, my father was on the spot to measure up for the repairs.'

Joining Uncle Sam

As well as working alongside the Americans, others actually worked for them, a suitable example of this being Des Fry and Alfred Harrison. Des was a native of the Dorset town of Weymouth, and a member of the local Home Guard platoon. His working ambition had been to enter the Dockyard Apprenticeship Scheme, but the war had altered things somewhat and instead he joined the Electrical Department at Bincleaves Royal Naval Torpedo Depot. Des and Alf worked in an area around the pier and quay that had been taken over by the Royal Navy, and named HMS *Bee*. Their electrical workshops were situated in what was the former pier ticket office. Weymouth would play an important part in America's contribution to the Normandy landings.

Des Fry explains in a little book about his life, titled *A Teenage View of Wartime Weymouth*, that on a Friday morning in 1943 he and Alf were called into the office of their chargeman Mr Harry Phillips and told that everything that was then under the control of HMS *Bee* was about to be taken over by the US Navy. The Americans had asked for two members of the electrical staff to be attached to them, under their control and discipline, and the management had decided that it should be Des and Alf.

The two men duly arrived the following Monday morning on their bikes at the main gate of what had previously been HMS *Bee*. The Americans had renamed the site USS *Grasshopper*. Here, they discovered that the normal sentry had been replaced by a representative of the US Navy, toting a machine carbine. After giving proof of their identity and purpose for being there, they were allowed to proceed to their workshop.

Within half an hour of their arrival, the two Brits were summoned over the tannoy system to see Lieutenant Saurte, the *Grasshopper*'s First Lieutenant. He immediately began to read them the riot act,

58 Nothe Fort (now a museum) guarded the embarkation of US troops from Weymouth in June 1944. (Photo: author)

suggesting that they had to fall in line, or else. At the end of a five-minute onslaught, Alf diffused what could have been a resentful start to their relationship by asking the man politely where he hailed from in America. This completely disarmed Lieutenant Saurte, who revealed that in civilian life he had been a lawyer in New York. Alf undoubtedly possessed the 'gift of the gab' and his diplomacy and tact was one of the reasons his British employers had chosen to send him.

The two men found themselves seconded to the CB Unit (Construction Battalion) or, as they became known to the film-going public, the 'Sea-Bees'. This was because of a popular movie called *The Fighting Sea-Bees*, which depicted America's method of enlisting entire construction firms into its Navy. At *Grasshopper*, Des and Alf worked with a firm from Texas, with four electricians on their staff. These were Bob Bolton, from El Paso, where his father owned a café. He could play the guitar and piano accordion, and would sing cowboy songs. Des used to think that, if he had a pair of six guns, he would be perfect for Hollywood. Then there was Smithy, or 'Smitty' as he was known. He was a super 'Mr Fix It', who could produce whatever was required, from a seemingly bottomless store. The third and youngest man was Mitchell, who was not much older than Des himself. Finally, there was Hank, who Des thinks was the oldest member of the team.

Weymouth Quay had previously been the mooring of Royal Navy Motor Torpedo and Gun Boats. These had now been replaced by Landing Craft Infantry (LCIs), in preparation for the invasion. These were the craft that would ferry men to the Normandy beaches on D-Day. Their crews were housed in Pulteney and Devonshire Buildings, replacing Royal Navy crews who had transferred to Portland or Portsmouth. At Weymouth Pavilion, mountains of American K rations began to build up, under the watchful eyes of armed sentries. These waterproofed cardboard boxes were filled with the food and other items that the soldiers would need when fighting in France. They were stacked up by a man with a forklift truck, something Alf and Des had never seen before.

Alexandra Gardens remained the mess hall but changed from providing separate mess rooms for different groups within the Royal Navy, such as petty officers, seamen, and marines, to one big canteen room, where all the Yanks messed together. Another innovation was the use, instead of plates for each course, of a stainless steel tray, with recesses to accommodate each part of the meal. This certainly made the chore of washing up much easier and, besides, the Americans possessed a dishwasher machine. The Sea Bees' workshops were filled with so many state-of-the-art tools and equipment that for Alf and Des it was like a wonderland, but what impressed Des most was their ability to organise things; there was no such word as 'can't' to the Americans.

Shortly afterwards a large khaki tent appeared on the promenade, which turned out to be a MASH unit staffed by surgeons, doctors, and their assistants, all under the command of a Major Cohen. At 10a.m. every working day Des and Alf, together with almost everyone else at the base, would descend on this tent for hot coffee and ring doughnuts, courtesy of the US Army. This unit attended to most medical needs of all the US forces in the Weymouth area.

Although the Americans had taken over the properties around the area of Weymouth Quay, the Royal Navy still retained a number of houses and hotels. Greenhill House (*The Grand Hotel*) was the WRNS Officer quarters under the command of a lady whom Des Fry would

59   American engineers in their working overalls. In this instance the 444th Sub Depot Engine Shop Crew at Molesworth. (Photo: courtesy of 303rd Bomb Group Association)

address as 'Ma'am Phillips'. He describes her as a very pleasant lady, who would offer them tea and biscuits, whenever they had to report to her about work in her buildings.

During the run up to Christmas 1943, Alf and Des were told that the WRNS intended putting on a stage show in the theatre ballroom of the *Burdon Hotel*. The couple were commissioned to arrange stage lighting for the show, and what happened next perfectly illustrates the resources that the Americans had available to them. The lady in charge was having two wooden platforms constructed on either side of the auditorium, on which she wanted the duo to mount spotlights.

'Where the dickens can we get hold of spotlights,' asked Alf. After all, it was the fourth year of the war. The Pavilion had previously been used as a gunnery training centre by the Royal Navy and was now a Yankie PX club and store. They scoured the dockyard, coming up with nothing, and although someone did offer an Aldis Signalling Lamp, the lady was adamant; she wanted four spotlights!

A day or so later, after bemoaning their failure to their American colleagues at coffee break, they returned to their workshop and outside they heard the honking of a horn. It was Smitty in a Jeep, with six battery-powered spotlights! Smitty said, 'Hop in Fry, and where's this *Burdon Hotel* you were on about?' 'Mr Fix It' had saved the day. The Wrens subsequently put on an entertaining show, complete with Can-Can dancers. Des took his sister Dorothy and Alf took his wife Doreen, and the event provided a little light relief in what Des describes as 'a pretty grey period of our existence'.

Earlier we learned of the large American ordnance depot at Charminster, a few miles from Dorchester. Apparently there were also British troops working on the site as well, one of which was Bill Gower, who, as a member of the Army Technicians Corps, found himself based at the REME depot. It was decided to attach one British officer and 12 technicians from Charminster to the American forces already gathered at Hamble near Southampton, to help prepare vehicles for D-Day.

None of them knew what to expect and, on arrival at the American camp, they were accommodated in two-man tents, with the officer enjoying one of his own. They effectively became GIs and joined the American chow line at meal times. Similar to Des Fry in Weymouth, Bill recalls being issued with a stainless steel tray with incised compartments for each part of the meal. As he and his friends shuffled along the line, they passed various food tables, at which orderlies continuously dished up the food. For breakfast there was a flapjack and bacon, with syrup poured over the lot; this was followed by cornflakes with either milk or cream; and finally pure white slices of bread. The tray became progressively fuller and heavier as you went down the line, but you could only hold it with one hand, as the other hand was needed for clutching a mug of coffee, which thankfully for the Brits was later changed to tea. And if that wasn't enough to manage, one of the orderlies would then lift up your arm and stick a quart tin of tomato juice in the armpit, while at the same time a folded copy of *Stars and Stripes* was pushed into the space between your neck and battledress blouse.

'The dinner,' Bill describes, 'was just as huge. A large piece of chicken was plonked on the tray, so big that it was dangling over the edges. There were potatoes, some kind of cabbage and gravy, followed by peaches and a large dollop of cream: then more coffee. Each meal was far too much for me to eat, but six months of this and for the first time in my life I had gained exactly one extra stone in body weight.'

The British had joined these American forces to monitor and service mechanical war vehicles, including radar vans and ack-ack guns. Part of their job was also to marshal all the traffic that saturated every road and lane in the eastern and southern counties of England. There were of course other small groups like theirs attached to other elements of the main invasion force. 'We like to think that although we did not take part in the D-Day landings,' Bill contemplates, 'we did our job well enough to avoid hold ups or delays.'

One of Bill's memories helps to illustrate the superior equipment that the Americans had at their disposal. His group had been detailed to take their British recovery truck and pull an ambulance out of a river, but the lane at the side of the river was so narrow that they were unable to swing their lifting jib around. They went back to camp and asked the GIs if they could borrow their 'wrecker', as they called it. 'Sure can,' they said, then one shouted to the others, 'Hey fellas Beeal [the name by which Bill had become known to them] has got an ambulance stuck, he needs some help.' With that half a dozen GIs swarmed around them. The wrecker was then driven down the narrow lane, stopped by the part-submerged ambulance, made the necessary attachments, swung its lifting jib round and successfully got the ambulance back on the road again.

In 1943 Cynthia Gray wanted to join the Women's Land Army or the Royal Navy, but, with one of her brothers fighting in France and the other a prisoner of the Japanese, her mother applied to the authorities on hardship grounds for her daughter to remain at home. So instead, Cynthia was directed to work for the American Army, and was sent to a depot called G30 – a warehouse in Commercial Road, Stepney, London. She would travel there each morning on the tube to Aldgate station, often seeing people sleeping on the platforms to be safe from the bombing.

During her time at the depot, Cynthia worked as a secretary for various officers, one of whom, a middle-aged married major, kept propositioning her and telling her not to go out with any enlisted men. She was actually dating an American sergeant at the time, and told the major that he was old enough to be her father. And besides, at only 22, how would he like his daughter to do what he wanted her to do?

The company of soldiers at the depot consisted of both northern and southern Americans, who Cynthia claims hated one another, even though they were all white. This situation led to numerous knife fights between them and kept the nearby police station very busy.

While at work the Americans were very efficient and ruthless in their business methods. They had no time for failure, valuing only achievement and success. They disliked English tea-breaks for instance, seeing them as a waste of valuable working time: they would simply have a bottle of Coke and keep on working. Each morning, everyone had to assemble and sing the American national anthem, although Cynthia herself kept her lips firmly shut!

Working in London there were of course moments of danger, and once doodlebugs landed nearby twice in the same day. She remembers some of the American girls being showered with glass as they looked out of the windows, and having their faces cut.

When the company moved to France, Cynthia's sergeant asked her to marry him and go back with him to his home in Tennessee after the war, but she declined in favour of remaining in England with her mother and friends.

OPPORTUNITIES FOR ALL

Many members of Britain's adult population were already engaged in some type of war work, but the arrival of the Americans brought opportunities to earn a little extra money on the side. For instance, while Tim Grace and the 368th Fighter Group were based at Greenham Common, a few luxuries at the camp came courtesy of an Englishman who became known as 'Black Market Joe'. One afternoon shortly after the group's arrival, he appeared at the Greenham Common living area, inviting people to purchase *The London Times* or *The Daily Mail*. His skinny figure, red, weather-beaten face, and shock of unruly silver hair soon became almost a permanent feature at the camp, selling items such as bouillon cubes, writing paper, bread and other essentials.

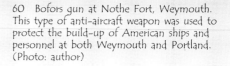

60 Bofors gun at Nothe Fort, Weymouth. This type of anti-aircraft weapon was used to protect the build-up of American ships and personnel at both Weymouth and Portland. (Photo: author)

61 For ladies who lived near an American base, there were many opportunities to make a little money by providing the men with a laundry service. In this photograph, GIs of the 392nd Bomb Group at Wendling appear to be hanging their smalls on a barbed-wire fence. (Photo: courtesy of www. b24.net)

Although there was a thriving black market in Britain, many people, especially women living near American bases, could offer services of a more legitimate nature, especially in terms of tailoring and laundry. Rosemary Robson lived in the village of Warmington near Oundle, where Americans of the 94th Combat Wing were based on the nearby airfield at Polebrook. Her father was a member of the Warmington Home Guard. Her mother was a tailoress and her parents' house, when she was growing up, was always cluttered with materials and sewing threads. Amongst all the clutter she recalls a large amount of parachute silk from which she would make petticoats or frilly, smocked dresses for her daughter. 'I remember her Sunday best blouse was made from this silk and beautifully smocked on the front and cuffs,' she says.

It appears that this parachute silk had been brought to her by airmen from Polebrook, and from it she would craft silk scarves, on to which she would embroider the emblem of the 8th USAAF. The airmen would send these scarves back to their families in the USA as gifts. But there was always plenty of silk left over for her personal use.

In Burnham on Sea in Somerset, Mrs J. Clarke was employed by Westman's Laundry and Dry Cleaners. 'We got to know many Americans both white and black,' she states, 'owing to seeing to their laundry and dry cleaning. They were very particular about their laundry and dry cleaning.'

One thing, she remembers, was being asked to arrange a trousers sponge and press for these men. They all wanted to have them done while they waited, so a room was made available upstairs in the laundry. Here they could climb out of their trousers and throw them down the stairs. It was then a question of waiting for them to be processed and returned. 'Of course they had no idea of the value of English money,' Mrs Clarke explains, 'they were still thinking in dollars.' The Americans would simply hold out a handful of money and say, 'Help yourself'.

After that, Mrs Clarke recalls that the Americans would spoil the working girls with chocolates and candy. 'We were once given a chicken in a tin to take home,' she furthers. 'We hadn't had such a thing for a

62   US Navy airmen queue up to use the public phone box, outside the old Post Office in Dunkeswell, Devon, where there was an American Navy airbase. Visitors to the village today will find that the scene has hardly changed: without the sailors, of course. (Photo: courtesy of Dunkeswell Memorial Museum)

long time and didn't we have a good dinner. We were invited to a dance at their airbase and were transported by lorry to Westonzoyland, and back home to Burnham free of charge. We were treated like royalty, and had doughnuts, coffee, oranges and bananas. These Americans were very lonely, thinking of their families far away, so to be invited to our homes was something very special.'

Mrs Clarke worked in an actual laundry business, but many other women provided a laundry service from their homes, especially if they had GIs billeted with them or they were accommodated in the neighbourhood. One such lady was the mother of Daphne Kellaway, who lived near a house in which officers had been billeted. Daphne isn't sure how the situation came about, but remembers it being hard work as her mother already had to look after four daughters and an ailing mother-in-law. Bear in mind also that, in the 1940s, few people had access to modern technology. All she had was a copper in the corner of the kitchen that needed a coal fire under it to heat the water. The water itself had to be poured into the copper from buckets and bowls. She took great pride in getting the whites really spotless, and shirts were perfectly ironed using an old-fashioned flat iron.

Back in Charminster in Dorset, Ivor Peters, who had earlier witnessed the arrival of the first American sentry box at the ordnance depot, was becoming very friendly with some of his new neighbours. He and the other village lads were allowed to walk in many parts of the camp, particularly the tented area where the troops were accommodated. This led one of the soldiers to ask him if there was anyone in the village that took in laundry. He made enquiries and discovered that a lady who lived near his house would be pleased to carry out this chore. This not only worked in her favour, but in Ivor's as well, as he would collect and deliver the laundry. He and a friend operated this laundry run with the aid of a wheelbarrow.

While visiting the camp on these regular laundry runs, Ivor became very familiar with the Americans. 'We never had any reason to fear being amongst these visitors,' he states, 'and I distinctly remember one soldier giving another a hard time for what today would be considered a very inoffensive remark. Once during a laundry collection, my pal and I were met by an American officer. His name has remained in my memory all these years – it was Captain Sweitzer. He looked and sounded like one of the gangsters from the films we watched in the cinema – a real tough guy – but we need not have worried, he only wanted his laundry tended to!'

Some of the Americans were very gullible and Mr R. Bennett, from Great Ashfield in Suffolk, remembers one pilot telling him that, on his first trip to London, when he got off at the train station some guy sold him a ticket to Petticoat Lane Market. Although they were well paid in comparison to British soldiers, they were paid monthly and were often broke long before the end of the month. At times like this, some of them would try to sell things to the locals in order to obtain some extra cash. Mr Bennett recalls one GI telling him that, after being paid on a Friday, he went to London and came back on Sunday with nothing. He'd spent his entire wage in a weekend, but his attitude was that he might have been dead on the Monday.

The necessity to find some extra cash, because some Americans had spent their wages too quickly, also meant that GIs themselves were often working Black Market rackets. For instance, when the Americans camped along the lanes near Reen Cross Farm, near Perranporth in Cornwall, Ronald Grubb recalls that at this time his father Arthur would walk to see his brother on the other side of the village, returning at about 9p.m. There was a complete blackout everywhere, when suddenly looming up in front of him were two large black soldiers, who offered him the purchase of a large bag of sugar. Being a little man and feeling slightly intimidated, he couldn't say no, so he took the sugar and gave them the money. But being a staunch Methodist, he felt uneasy about the transaction, feeling that he was wrong to have accepted. So he hid the sugar in the hedgerow, covering it with

63 Sheila Pitman's father worked as a storeman at the American Army hospital in Axminster. He is seen here, on the left, with personnel including Curtis (2nd from right) who was a regular visitor to their home. (Photo: Courtesy of Sheila Pitman)

grass and returned the following morning, in daylight, with his horse and cart. Putting the sugar in the cart and covering it well, the only justification for his act was the fact that, in a time of rationing, everything including sugar was in short supply.

On another farm, but in Dorset, it was the local scrumpy cider that the Americans got a taste for. Ellice Hansford and her husband Ernie were married on 15 October 1939 and took over a small farm called Kingsland Farm at Salwayash near Bridport. They started out with only five cows, ten pigs and a horse and cart. However, after the arrival of Americans in the area, they quickly discovered that a searchlight unit was employed a little way up the road. Her husband paid them a visit, and made arrangements to collect their swill each morning with the horse and cart. This swill was basically all of their waste food collected in containers, which he took back to the farm and boiled – compulsory by law – and mixed with barley meal, to feed to the pigs.

The farm also boasted two apple orchards, and they were able to produce many gallons of cider in their own cider mill. The American lads soon got to hear of this and it wasn't long before Ernie was also carrying a barrel of good old 'English scrumpy cider' on the cart, when he went to get the swill. The Americans loved it!

'Of course,' Mrs Hansford points out, 'they could not have the cider without some payment and back would come a huge tin of corned beef, a large lump of cheese, or a large tin of sliced peaches. As rationing was

64   The late Arthur Paul Grubb, with Tinker the horse and Bob the dog, at Reen Cross Farm near Perranporth in 1945. (Photo: courtesy of Ronald Grubb)

on we were overjoyed as we now had two children. They were lovely lads, the Yanks, always polite and well mannered and I expect the pub up there did well from them as well. It was called the *Gallop Arms* but is now closed. Happy days! I will never forget those lovely handsome American boys who came to our farm and often helped out, picking up apples, haymaking, feeding the pigs, or milking the cows.'

As the Americans seemed to have plenty of ready money and a willingness to spend every penny of it, local shops also did a roaring trade. This even applied to specialist shops that had suffered during the early stages of the war.

When Ivor Strange left school at 14, which coincided with the period when the Yanks were billeted in Dorchester, he went to work for C. Jeffery and Sons, Bespoke Gunsmiths, in High East Street, just opposite the Corn Exchange, itself the scene of many wartime jives. To the Americans, with their national gun culture, this shop was like a magnet. The owner at the time, Mr Ronald Jeffery, apart from being a master gunsmith, was also the chief of the town's Fire Brigade, a town councillor, a Justice of the Peace and Dorchester's mayor through most of the war.

During the D-Day build up, Ivor notes that the gun shop was a hive of activity, and the Americans were always impressed by his knowledge of firearms, most of which he admits to learning from Ronald Jeffery. One particular friend was Lieutenant Attaya, from New England, who was a fanatic gun collector. He was billeted in the Old Shire Hall, High West Street, the site of Judge Jeffreys Bloody Assizes. He often invited Ivor to Sunday tea in the quarters he shared with five other young officers. Cakes, coffee, peaches and cream or ice-cream were all available from the kitchen downstairs.

Under his mattress, Lieutenant Attaya kept quite an arsenal of rifles and pistols, and in his locker there was even a complete Lewis Gun. In time he managed to have this entire collection shipped back to the States, courtesy of Uncle Sam. Mind you, Ivor himself was very disappointed when Mr Jeffery sold him some of his own personal favourites, including, he says, 'my pet, a Marlin 30-30 rifle'. But also many others, such as a matched pair of Derringers and his favourite Mauser hunting rifle. Attaya's unit was eventually shipped out to Weymouth for the invasion, and Ivor has no further knowledge of him, or whether or not he was ever reunited with his precious collection.

Eric Puckett also left school at 14 and went to work as an apprentice saddler, to the business of Miles Saddler, situated in High West Street, Dorchester, although he had been working there as a Saturday boy since he was twelve. This shop proved to be another magnet to the Americans who loved anything made of leather. He remembers being kept very busy making watch straps, wide belts for dispatch riders and leather tops for boots. He also made shoulder holsters, as many of the GIs had their own private revolvers. No doubt Lieutenant Attaya made an appearance in the shop at some point. 'Everything was hand stitched,' relates Mr Puckett with pride, 'and they loved to come into the workshop to watch us. I made quite a bit of pocket money by stitching belts etc. at home.'

65   Soldiers of the 4th Armored Division with Red Cross ladies outside the American Red Cross Service Club in Devizes. Bill Underwood and his brother, who lived in Devizes, would be taken to the camp daily to cut the men's hair. (Photo: courtesy of Elsie Lewis)

Bill Underwood's father ran a barber's shop in Old Sheep Street, Devizes, where both Bill, who was then 14, and his elder brother Geoff, aged 16, worked. The shop was well patronised by troopers from the 4th Armored Division after they arrived at Devizes camp. Shortly afterwards a young American officer came into the shop and asked Mr Underwood if he would send the two boys out to the camp to cut the soldiers' hair. He agreed, and every day a Jeep would arrive to pick up the boys. This went on for several weeks until they found American servicemen able to take over the job.

'We used to charge one shilling for a haircut during the war,' recalls Bill. 'We were amazed to hear the swearing of these soldiers. My father never swore and it was quite an eye opener for us.' This last statement adds to our confusion about the character of the Americans, as we have already read a couple of accounts stating that the GIs were careful with their language around children. However, it helps to emphasise the fact that these soldiers weren't all the same, everyone was an individual. We have also to bear in mind that, in the 1940s, you were already of working age at 14 and consequently treated like an adult.

Chapter 5

Men and Machines

From the spring of 1942 onwards, thousands of American servicemen began to arrive in Britain, bringing with them the machines needed to defeat their enemies in Europe. These men and machines became a very visible part of the British landscape, especially the different types of aircraft that almost at once began their attacks on continental targets. Daily bombing runs often filled the skies close to these airbases, and people living beneath their flight path were constantly aware of their presence. Even in the most rural locations, if an airbase sprang up nearby, the local people were no longer on the war's periphery, they were in the thick of it.

On the ground, thousands of vehicles of every shape and size trundled into the West Country in the months before D-Day. Huge tanks and trucks manoeuvred down the tiny lanes of Dorset, Devon and Cornwall. At locations such as the Charminster Depot, vehicles were constantly on the move, as they were prepared for action in the European battlefields. At Weymouth and other places along the south coast, large tracts of land became holding car parks, where men and machines waited for the order to 'go'.

Doing the job

But what was it like for the American servicemen themselves, working in Britain's back yard? They were here to do a job, and the location at which they did it was in some ways irrelevant, as long as it enabled them to attack their foe. Whit Hill told us earlier about living conditions at Bassingbourn in Cambridgeshire, nicknamed 'The Country Club'. He was serving there as a Sheet Metal Crew Chief with the 91st Bomb Group, working on B-17 Flying Fortresses.

Each day the aircrews departed in their 'ships' on missions over occupied Europe, while the ground staff worked on British soil, making certain that the aircraft in their charge were prepared for action and safe to fly.

Whit Hill describes the responsibilities of the ground staff, explaining: 'They were always there before the flight crews arrived, way before sun up on the morning of mission days, to ensure their aircraft were in top condition. It made no difference that they may have worked half the night correcting discrepancies noted by the last pilot who flew the plane, or fixing up the last mission battle damage such as the electrician repairing severed electrical wires etc. When Ground Crews first arrived

66 Brand new B-17G models produced at one of Boeing's plants await final painting and check-out. This one was number 5,000 as it rolled off the final assembly line. Note that each employee was allowed to paint his/her name on the fuselage, etc. That's the way it was delivered to the 8th Air Force in England. (Photo: copyright Paul Chryst)

at their aircraft on mission days, they would make a cursory walk-around inspection of their aircraft and grounds to insure nothing had been touched since the last time they were there. Generally the only ones who visited the bombers in the middle of the night were the Bomb Loaders who had to wait until the mission details for the type of bomb load the aircraft would be carrying.'

Having checked outside his aircraft, the crew chief and his assistant would run through numerous essential pre-flight checks. These included extracting any oil from the cylinders that might have collected overnight; opening the fuel petcocks located under the wings in order to drain off any water that might have accumulated in the tanks; checking the brakes; making sure there were no restrictions in the operation of the wing and tail elevators, and tail rudder; starting and checking all four engines; lowering and raising the flaps; opening and closing the bomb bay doors; and testing the windscreen wipers. Then there were other checks, such as making sure the aircraft had toilet paper aboard.

After all these checks had been carried out, the ground crew considered the aircraft was ready for its mission. It was now time for the combat crew to arrive, who would carry out their own sets of tasks, such as installing the Norton Bomb Sight; plotting their route; inserting the 50-calibre guns; hooking up the ammunition tracks and checking oxygen lines. When all this had been done, the ground crew would clear the area in front of the propellers, the pilot would start his engines, the wheel chocks would be removed, and the aircraft would taxi away ready for take off.

Once the aircraft had departed, the ground crews would be able to go to the mess hall for breakfast, or even catch up with some sleep. Whit Hill poignantly remembers the moment, later in the day, when the squadron would return home to Bassingbourn.

'Later in the day the ETA of the mission would be announced. The ground crews biked or walked out to the tower area to watch the Group's aircraft return. If the aircraft returned in a ragged formation or with empty spaces, the men knew it had been a rough mission. As each bomber landed it was met by its ground crew at its dispersal area parking pad. Those bombers that had injured crews, taxied up to the tower, where medics and ambulances were at the ready. The ground crews and medics wasted no time to get inside the aircraft and give assistance to the injured. The medics had the tough job of retrieving and taking the dead corpses to the morgue. Once the casualties were removed, the Crew Chief and his assistant would taxi the bomber back to the proper dispersal area. In the case of serious injuries, a medical unit came down to the aircraft to clean it up. At the pads, the bombers were inspected for battle damage, and estimates were made as to how long it would take to have the aircraft operational again. If

67   The heroes of Flight Line Maintenance: 91st Bomb Group (Heavy) Bassingbourn. (Photo: copyright Paul Chryst)

the damages were small, sheet metal crews would work all night if necessary to have them ready for a mission the next morning.'

Of course, there were often ground crews waiting for aircraft that simply didn't return. The men waited and waited, hoping for any news of their ship. Perhaps it had made an emergency landing at another base nearby. 'They waited with their bicycles near the tower,' explains Whit Hill, as he vividly describes the scene. 'Some sitting on their seats with one leg on the ground, others standing with the bicycle between their legs, and others standing with the bicycle leaning against their back, not saying much, but hoping for the best. As the darkness fell so did the hopes of their aircraft and crew returning. The fuel supply only lasted so long. Slowly they rode off to their quarters in subdued silence. While they may not have shown emotion, they were indeed grieved over the loss of the young men they had shaken hands with earlier that day.'

But what of the pilots themselves, who had arrived fresh from training in America, into what was effectively a war zone? George Rarey's letters home to his wife Betty Lou give a good indication of the situation facing these young men. Rarey of course was a fighter, rather than a bomber pilot, serving with 379th Fighter Squadron, who in late 1943 found themselves at Wormingford near Colchester in Essex. In this letter, Rarey shows his frustration at the situation where they had come to England to fight, but there were no planes for them to fly, so further training filled their days.

Another day of nothing in particular. Lordy, but we'd like to have some airplanes! We're learning a lot but we miss the flying quite a bit. Today was typical – here it is. As far as breakfast was concerned we were in the weeds because we grabbed an extra 30 minutes of sacktime. Our first class was at 9:00. They are informal affairs, these classes. Lectures by experienced men in our Air Force as well as in the RAF. Interesting. At 12:00 we knocked off for lunch which consisted in a sort of hash, potatoes, and I forget what else. After about an hour of loafing around the fire in the lounge, back to the old schoolroom. Class was interrupted when a Mosquito night fighter gave us a good buzz job. That is a beautiful aircraft. We got quite a thrill out of it. I'm beginning to feel like a groundpounder. Sure will feel good to feel that old prop pulling you along again. I didn't realise how much I could miss flying. School was out at 4:00. Threw on a blouse and then to dinner after two bottles of very good ale in the lounge.

While still waiting for planes to arrive the squadron underwent more and more training, including exercises around the British countryside, practising escape and evasion techniques. What to do if you were shot down over enemy territory. All of the pilots were taken out in their normal flight gear early in the morning in a completely covered truck, so they couldn't keep track of where they were going. They were then let out, two at a time somewhere in the countryside. They were given maps of the area, and their goal was to make it back to the base without being apprehended. Apparently, they were told it was OK to 'steal' any type of transportation available. Their pursuers on the day were the local Home Guard platoon, alerted to their presence and with orders to capture them. Airmen were also posted around the base perimeter, to stop them gaining entry. The maps were useful but hard to follow as for some time all road signs in that part of Britain had been taken

68   George Rarey's depiction of the mayhem caused in the quiet English countryside when the squadron took part in an escape and invasion exercise. (Illustration: courtesy of Linda Rarey and the EAA Museum)

down or obliterated, in order to confuse any invading forces. With the legal theft of several British cars and trucks, the exercise couldn't have done a lot of good for Anglo-American relations and, to top it all, it seems that none of the pilots actually made it back to the camp within the established deadline.

The squadron pilots also went to Ipswich swimming baths to practise dinghy survival training, just in case they were shot down into the North Sea. But in December, they finally received their first batch of P-47s. Soon they were in regular action over France, and the following extract paints an atmospheric picture of how the English countryside helped to ease the pilots into sleep.

> It's just dusk and we've finished chow and put another day behind us. Through the open tent flap I can see the pleasant English countryside stretching away to the gray misty horizon. The smoke from the many tents hangs low in this little cup of land. You can hear snatches of conversations from the various tents – the clank of the mess kits as the men come in from late chow. Some guy is playing a harmonica and a little old bird is singing his wonderful fool heart out. I'm tired and I've come to the part of the day I like most. You're with me always, but this time in the half light between day and night always seems sort of special.

From the evidence of many Americans who served in England, it is obvious that they fell in love with the place and its people. It must have been very special to return from a long, dangerous flight deep over enemy territory to the pretty green fields and wooded vales of England, and to that first pint of beer in the local village pub.

From bomber and fighter pilots, we turn our attention to fliers of quite a different sort, which nevertheless did an important job of their own for the US Army. David Hay lived with his family on Stoke Hill Farm, at Stoke village near Andover in Hampshire, where, incidentally, the Americans played baseball in a large meadow. The farm he says is 500 feet above sea level and US Army carrier pigeons were trained there. As far as he is aware, all of the Army's pigeons, which were later used in France, were trained on this one spot. The pigeon lofts were kept on the farm itself, but the two officers in charge, Lieutenants Salz and Eckenroth, were billeted at Tidworth. The two men spent Christmas 1943 on the farm, which they enjoyed very much. The evidence of this is a letter signed by Erwin Salz, dated 27 December 1944, and sent to Mrs Hay from the 'Signal Pigeon Center, APO 298, US Army', which reads:

> My Dear Mrs Hay,
> Hope you will excuse the belated arrival of this note of 'thank you', it is none the less sincere. To say thank you will not begin to express the gratitude Lt. Eckenroth and myself feel after sharing the warmth of a real home Christmas with your family.
> I wish it had been possible for all the troops far from home to have had a similar experience.
> Will call you early in the New Year and arrange to bring a loft of performing pigeons to your hill top.

American servicemen were doing all sorts of jobs in Britain. They weren't simply here to train for the fighting in Europe. Many had practical jobs to do, such as building camps and airfields, or the slipways mentioned on the river Dart. Others worked at the ordnance depots servicing military vehicles. Frank Kidwell told us about his friend, James Owens, who worked in the Rail Transportation Office at Barnstaple. Similarly, Joyce Beard, currently a parish councillor for Burnham Without, recalls the RTO Office at Highbridge in Somerset:

'During the Second World War, Americans who were billeted in homes in Highbridge worked at the railway station keeping petrol going to the front. A Railway Transportation Office was housed in one of these buildings, previously built as a large engine repair works in 1862 alongside the river Brue. It was established in 1942 and used until November 1945. All troop movements in this area were made through this Office. The US personnel were also responsible for a large petrol, oil and lubrication depot located on the site.'

IN THE LINE OF FIRE

For those who lived near an American airbase, the sight of aircraft leaving and returning each day has become one of the most evocative memories of those long years of war. Walter Perry lived near the airfield at Ridgewell and notes: 'Often when we came out of school the B-17s were returning from their day bombing missions. Several had engines not in use and showing the visible scars of their conflict over Germany. The aircraft would fire off flares before landing indicating dead or wounded on board or that the aircraft was damaged. As young children we thought it was unfair that all undamaged aircraft were to land first, but of course the reality was that a crippled B-17 would clog up the runway for the others.'

At Dereham in Norfolk Tony Blades has similar memories of aircraft returning to Shipdham: 'We would watch the planes return from their

69   David Hay and his older brother at the American Army pigeon lofts that were set up on their parents' farm near Andover. (Photo: courtesy of Dr David Hay)

70   This cartoon by George Rarey shows us how he set about painting the cowlings of the aircraft in his squadron. (Illustration: courtesy of Linda Rarey and the EAA Museum)

daylight bombing raids or missions. One or two of the planes would sometimes be limping and sometimes some never returned at all. We used to count them going out and coming home. Even as a youngster I found it very touching as each crew member jumped down and kissed the ground of England. All planes were named and had a painting usually of a partly clad female, the one that sticks in my mind was *Pregnant Peg*.'

Of course during his time off, cartoonist George Rarey would often relax by painting nose art images on the cowlings of the 379th Squadron P-47s. And contrary to the common perception that all nose art depicted half-naked women, most of Rarey's customers had a preference for animals. In one of his letters he wrote:

> Painted some cowlings this afternoon – have about half of them finished. It is a colorful thing to see the old 379th lined up for take off – looks like a menagerie. It sort of gives personality to an otherwise pretty cold collection of machinery. I think it means quite a bit to the pilots, and the crews that keep the planes in shape get a kick out of them, too – and I enjoy doing it, a pretty good thing all round.

In 1943 a new airfield was built at Eye in Suffolk for the 490th Bomb Group, who employed both B-24s and B-17s during their stay. Geoff Bartrum lived only 440 yards away from the base, so he became quite intimate with the various aircraft that came and went. 'On 23 April 1944,' he explains, 'the first planes landed. These were bombers and a few Mustang fighters. We children soon adopted a plane to follow the fortunes of, watching it take off for missions and looking out for it to return. They mostly had nose art on them. The one I followed had a picture of Huckleberry Duck painted on it.'

Living close to an airbase often put people in a position of extreme danger. After all, the Americans were engaged in wartime missions that

71   Examples of 379th Squadron cowlings painted by George Rarey. The men in the squadron had a preference for cartoon animals, which made the artist write: 'It is a colorful thing to see the old 379th lined up for take off – looks like a menagerie. It sort of gives personality to an otherwise pretty cold collection of machinery.' (Photos: courtesy of the EAA Museum)

resulted in many unfortunate incidents, which their British neighbours were likely to witness or be affected by. This was particularly true, if an airplane crashed on take off, or while returning home.

The evidence of this is sometimes recorded in memorials dotted around the country, such as one in the churchyard at Ashdon, Essex, where a plaque is dedicated to the memory of Mrs Elizabeth Everitt, a local farmer's wife, who saw an A-20 Havoc of the 409th Bomb Group crash in a field during 1944. She attempted to rescue the crew but the blazing aircraft exploded killing them and Mrs Everitt. She is also commemorated in the tower at Little Walden, the airfield from which the A-20 took off.

At Freckleton in Lancashire there is a memorial playground constructed by American servicemen and opened on 21 August 1945. It also incorporates an ornamental garden with a plaque reading: 'This playground presented to the children of Freckleton by their American neighbours of Base Air Depot No 2 USAAF in recognition and remembrance of their common loss in the disaster of Aug. 23 1944.' In the entrance to Freckleton School is a plaque listing the names of two teachers and 38 pupils who were killed. The aircraft was a B-24H Liberator which crashed whilst trying to land at nearby Warton in a thunderstorm. The three crewmen were also killed in what was the worst flying accident in Britain during the war.

At Tibenham, Dorothy Knapp remembers counting the planes as they left the airbase. 'When they came back,' she says, 'pieces were missing from the wings and tails, or engines were stopped. We often wondered how many made it home. Sometimes they crashed on take off. I used to get very upset. I can remember when two collided one foggy morning. Some of the wreckage came down in a field where I now live. There was a very tall tree near the camp which the Americans used as a lookout, but the Iron platform they had at the top of it, had just fallen down.'

Eric Peachey lived a couple of miles from the airfield at Rougham in Suffolk, and the flight path of its B-17s took them straight overhead. 'At 7.30 one morning in July,' he notes, 'one crashed a mile from our house, and all its bombs exploded at once. There was terrible damage to many properties in the village of Thurston, including to the church and school. The B-17 was called *Little Boy Blue* and seven of the crew were killed.'

But it wasn't only the crashes themselves that created danger for local people, it was also the debris they left strewn over the countryside. Eric Peachey remembers how children would forage near a crash site to pick up any live ammunition they could find, from which they would remove the cordite by pouring it out in a long line, and then set light to it. On one occasion Eric and his friends put the empty cartridges of a 50-calibre gun into a fire, some of which exploded and one of the firing caps entered his left thigh, leaving a neat round hole. At another site they found a damaged verey light pistol, and some cartridges, which they began to fire, until the local police found out about it, with the

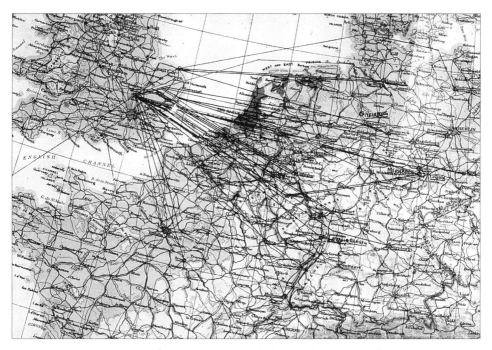

72   Large Mercator map of Europe kept by Lt Paul Chryst on his barracks wall at Bassingbourn, England, during his combat tour with the 91st BG (H) from July to December 1944. The black drawn lines indicate the actual flight routes to and from the bombed targets. This same map now hangs on display in the World War II section of the USAF (USAAF) Museum in Dayton, Ohio. (Illustration: copyright Paul Chryst)

consequence that the young 14-year-old appeared in court, but was subsequently let off with a warning.

At Great Yeldham in Essex, very near the airbase at Ridgewell, Jean Angel recalls that, as the Americans were involved in daylight bombing, they became used to hearing them going off in the morning as they were getting ready for school. 'On one occasion,' she writes, 'I can remember there was a huge explosion which shook the house and we heard that an aircraft fully laden with bombs had come down in a local wood with no survivors. We could see the bombers returning at around tea time, some were limping, many with holes in their wings and body.'

One day, the lesson at the village school was interrupted when a 'huge' black soldier came into the classroom to say that he had a lorry outside the building with a full load of bombs on board, with its engine on fire. 'We all rushed to the air raid shelter in the school grounds,' says Jean, 'though not one of us would have survived if the bombs had exploded, as the shelter was nearer to the burning lorry than the school.'

Joy Matthews, who lived near the aerodrome at Eye in Suffolk recalls an incident when a B-17 killed a roadman as it came in to land. The wing of the plane cut his horse in half. 'Us kids were more concerned about the horse than the poor man,' she admits. And on another night a returning plane crash-landed on a bomb dump causing a huge explosion. People nearby could hear the cries of the crew. 'Incidentally,' she points out, 'the bomb dump was nearer to the civilian population of the village than it was to the crew's quarters. We were actually in more danger from US aircraft than anything that Jerry threw at us.'

A training exercise led to a lifelong quest for Fred Carr who as a boy lived on the Larkman Estate in Norwich. At the time Fred, who was 16, witnessed the dramatic flight in which a four-engined Liberator bomber came close to demolishing his home and most of Beecherno Road.

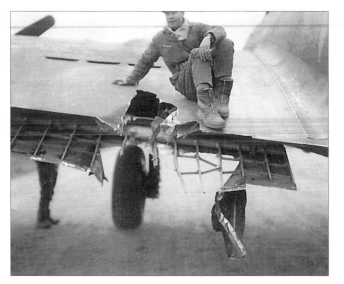

73 Mission damage caused to the wing of B-17G Bam Bam, while on a mission to Frankfurt with the 303rd Bomb Group on 29 January 1944. (Photo: courtesy of 303rd Bomb Group Association)

He saw the bomber, on a test flight from Horsham St Faith, sweep across the Larkman at barely more than rooftop height. Fred didn't think the aircraft was going to make it across the estate as it appeared to be coming down. The final house in the Liberator's path was his own, which it missed by inches, before finally pancaking in a nearby field. Fred recalled it as a 'perfect crash-landing. There was no fire.' This made a lasting impression on the 16-year-old.

The pilot of the aircraft was Fred O'Neill, who managed to walk away from the crash unscathed. The only other man on the plane suffered a nose injury. His brave handling of the situation, and decision to remain with the aircraft until it landed, almost certainly prevented civilian loss of life: or at very least serious damage to the properties below. For this, the residents of the Larkman Estate threw a party in his honour and presented O'Neill with a commemorative clock in gratitude.

Fred Carr, who was an air cadet at the time, didn't get the chance to thank O'Neill himself, and later in life he became interested in tracking the pilot down. The quest took 20 years to complete. Eventually, 40 years after the event, through the help of aviation enthusiasts, Fred Carr discovered O'Neill's address in Philadelphia and wrote, thanking him for his courage and consideration.

The reply was swift and in it a surprised Colonel O'Neill recalled the flight. 'Everything was OK at 900ft over Norwich. Suddenly, dead silence. All four engines quit. I am very glad to hear we didn't hit your dad's chimney because I well remember a roof and chimney directly ahead of me before we pancaked.'

He also revealed that the clock that he was given by the people of Norwich was still ticking away and in pride of place in his home. Fred Carr and his wife became good friends with Fred O'Neill and his wife, and they exchanged many visits until the ex-pilot's eventual death.

Roy Mellor, whose father was a police sergeant in Bury St Edmunds, also recalls a training flight that went terribly wrong, in this instance killing numerous crew members. It was 5 January 1945 at around 2.30p.m., and Roy notes that the day in question was cold but bright, with a clear blue sky. Two B-17 bombers of the 490th Bomb Group from Eye were approaching Bury on a training flight when they collided over the north-eastern outskirts of the town.

'I was off school owing to illness,' explains Roy, 'and was looking out from the window of our top floor flat, and suddenly spotted parachutes descending and pieces of aircraft wreckage fluttering down like so much tinfoil. When my father finished duty that night, he told me one bomber had crashed at Hall Farm, Fornham St Martin, and the other into one of the settling lagoons at the sugar beet factory.'

Of those on board the two aircraft, only three survived, with 16 men losing their lives. Some of the bodies were soon recovered from the lagoon and two floated to the surface eight days later. One crew member had crashed through the glass roof of the sugar beet factory, which left only one victim to be accounted for. He was found some days later in melting snow near the factory gate by two lads from nearby Holderness Road. Roy suggests that, although most of the wreckage was cleared soon after, pieces of one aircraft still lie buried at Hall Farm to this day.

These frequent aircraft crashes naturally supply an abundance of gruesome anecdotes. For instance, Ron Green remembers the morning he was walking to school at Wymondham in Norfolk, with his mother and two sisters, when a formation of Flying Fortresses passed overhead. One of the aircraft was on fire and moving slowly towards the ground. His mother prayed for parachutes but none appeared. Finally the plane twisted and plummeted into some trees between Wicklewood and Morley, and there was a mighty explosion followed by the sound of bullets, lasting for quite some time. Some time later at school, his friend Alan Roberts said that his father had found an arm in a tree, and on it was a watch that was still ticking.

At Charminster, near the ordnance depot, Ivor Peters admits that, although life was great fun for most of the time for children, there was also a serious aspect regarding the American occupation of the site. The lane that ran past the camp for about a mile was lined on either side by military stores most of which were munitions. German bombers en route to Bristol would invariably be intercepted by British fighter planes, and any German aircraft that turned back would jettison its bomb load anywhere it could. So there was always the danger of the camp being hit on these occasions. Obviously, if the Germans knew about the site, it would have been a target in its own right. Had it been attacked, the consequences for the village would have been devastating. Ivor explains that there were also anti-aircraft guns scattered around the camp, and when these went into action it was very frightening for the local population.

THE SCARS OF WAR

As well as the scars created by the enemy activity that the American presence attracted, there were also visible scars that the Americans caused themselves. Norton Fitzwarren in Somerset was of course the

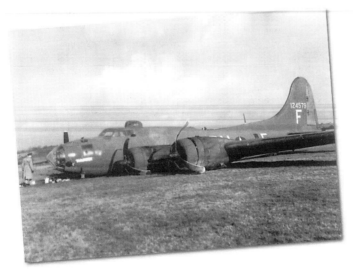

74 B-17F Thumper, of the 303rd Bomb Group, following a crash landing at Lulsgate Bottom on 23 January 1943. (Photo: courtesy of 303rd Bomb Group Association)

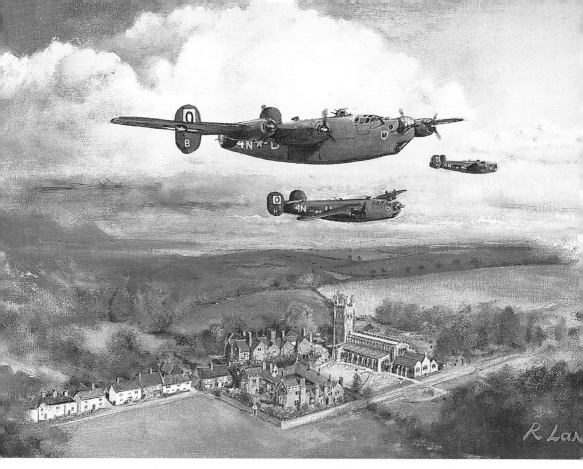

75 This painting by Roger Lane, 'Liberators over Long Melford', depicts B-24s of the 486th Bomb Group from Sudbury, and shows perfectly the fact that aircraft, either departing from or arriving at their bases, flew over villages and residential areas. (Reproduced with the permission of Roger Lane)

location of the G50 stores depot near Taunton, and from the parish council minutes, Mary Hayward provides the following:

> 20th April 1944: Rose Cottage – Mr Moor asked support of the Council in his effort to allow the wall to be taken down and put further back at Rose Cottage, the Americans having damaged it repeatedly and in his estimation it was a danger spot for children. The chairman reported having discussed the matter with the Rural District Council, whose reply was definitely 'No improvements in war time.'
>
> 2nd October 1944: Rose Cottage – Mr Pallett reported attempts to improve the corner at Rose Cottage and the Chapel Corner, to be negatived [sic] by the County Council, stating 'No improvements in war time.'

The road outside Rose Cottage was very narrow with a sharp bend, and Mary assumes that the constant damage was caused by Americans coming around the corner too fast and hitting the garden wall.

It's not surprising that the Americans caused a certain amount of damage, when we consider the quantity of military vehicles that must have been travelling around West Country lanes at this time. At the Charminster depot, Ivor Peters watched keenly at the incredible growth of the site. He was thrilled to see all the wonderful vehicles that travelled through this quiet Dorset village. 'Names like Mack, GMC, Chrysler and Dodge became familiar for trucks and cars. The favourite was the Willys Jeep – we had never seen anything like them and they sped about everywhere. As children we did not really know what was happening but in due course we learnt that this camp was one of many in the south of England preparing for the invasion of Europe.'

Trucks of all sizes and shapes went through Charminster, as well as tanks, amphibious vehicles (called DUKWs), mobile cranes, tank transporters, Jeeps, personnel carriers, motorcycles and staff cars. Many of these vehicles were being prepared to withstand the perils of both the sea journey and the physical assault on the beaches of Normandy.

One very sad incident at Charminster occurred one night when a medium-sized American truck failed to negotiate a hairpin bend just outside the village. The vehicle overturned and the driver lay trapped during the night – he died as a result of his injuries.

Not that far away, at Stoborough on the Isle of Purbeck, London evacuee Peter Tamplin also witnessed the build-up of vehicles and men. Placed midway between Poole Harbour and the Bovington Tank Ranges, many different units arrived in the area for training. Next to Stoborough Primary School was a marshy field, separated by a narrow brook. Tanks and transporters were placed in the field prior to D-Day. Then, following a very wet night, these huge transporters sought to leave the field and immediately sank to their axles. In the end they had to use tanks to pull the transporters free and in doing so ploughed up the road surface. They eventually left the field with very red faces, to a chorus of youthful catcalls from the watching school children.

The obvious dangers to children that these large vehicles posed, as predicted by Mr Moor at Norton Fitzwarren, became a reality in Andover,

76   Visible scars left to property as a B–17G skids and crashes into a hangar at Molesworth on 9 December 1944. (Photo: courtesy of 303rd Bomb Group Association)

Hampshire, although the incident remembered by Jane Bedmanzyk didn't prove too serious. Andover was surrounded by a number of army or air corps camps, so the Americans created a lot of traffic in the town. 'Large lorries brought men through our streets,' writes Jane, 'their Jeeps sped dramatically from the railway station down the Junction Road. An encounter with individual American servicemen was a cheery one – they were friendly, generous and particularly charming towards children. Still, they were much resented in Andover which they seemed to "occupy" in spite of their good manners.'

Jane's father was a member of an Andover firm of builders and, when wartime regulations prevented him from continuing to build private houses, he accepted a job locally with the War Department. This is why he was at home at the time of the incident in question, as he walked Jane and her younger sister to school one morning.

'On the way to school,' Jane recalls, 'my impetuous little sister decided to drop father's hand and make an independent dash across the Junction Road. A Yankee Jeep was, as usual, speeding along it. They saw my sister and halted just in time. Their radiator barely touched her and she was completely unharmed, although no doubt shaken.'

The two men in the Jeep jumped out, picked the little girl up, and dusted her down. She seemed to be OK, and they apologised profusely to her father. 'Typically', Jane states, her father in return apologised to them for his daughter's naughtiness. They asked for his address so that they might visit the following day, to check on the little girl's recovery. Reluctantly the man agreed thinking it to be, 'a lot of unnecessary fuss!'

The two men duly arrived the next day as promised, bringing with them an army captain, who greatly impressed Jane's mother with his gallantry 'and smart uniform'. The two men unloaded the Jeep and carried into the kitchen enough household commodities to cover the dresser. 'I particularly remember the tinned meats, and bars of wonderful soap,' says Jane. 'Oh, and oranges which ran along the shelf and had to be collected by us children to keep them safe.'

From Jane's and various other accounts, it becomes evident that GIs enjoyed speeding around the countryside in their Jeeps, giving little consideration to people, animals, and dangerous road conditions. It seems hypocritical, therefore, that Bill Gower was reprimanded for driving too fast in the confines of an American camp. Bill of course was serving with the Army Technicians Corps at the REME depot at Charminster, but had been detailed to go to the American camp at Blandford. He was driving a British truck, when suddenly an American Jeep passed him and waved him down to a stop. Two American military policemen got out of the vehicle, telling him to get down from his driver's seat. They proceeded to inform him that he had exceeded the 15 MPH speed limit inside their camp. Bill didn't argue the point and made an apology, which they chose to ignore. They asked him his name and serial number.

'I was a bit hesitant in my reply,' Bill recalls, 'because I did not understand what they meant by "your serial." So one of them wrote down the number painted on my truck.' It then occurred to Bill that

77 Members of the 430th Anti-Aircraft Artillery Automatic Weapons Battalion (Mobile), with some of their equipment, at Barwick Park, Yeovil in Somerset. (Photo: courtesy of Graham Toms)

they might have meant his army number. He tried to quote this, but the MP closed his book and put it in his pocket. They sent him on his way, warning him to observe the speed signs in future.

After Bill had finished his duties at Blandford he drove back to Charminster, where within an hour of his return he was summoned into the sergeant major's office and informed that he had to go back to Blandford to answer a charge that had been made against him. He was taken back to the American camp by the duty car and driver, and on arrival at Blandford was marched into the American commander's office by the same two MPs that had previously stopped him. Inside, three other American officers were also waiting, in what appeared to be a formal hearing.

Bill continues the story by explaining: 'The American commander told me that I was on a charge for knocking down one of his soldiers with my truck. I tried to explain that I hadn't knocked anyone down, but he looked down at the paper on his desk and said, "Your name is Glover isn't it?" I told him that it wasn't Glover, but Gower! He looked at the paper again and said, "Your serial number is," and then quoted the truck number. I replied, "No sir, this is my serial number" and I showed him my army pay book. He insisted: "You knocked down one of my soldiers." Again, I explained that I hadn't knocked anyone down and that, as far as I was aware, the only reason I had been stopped by his MPs was for exceeding the 15MPH speed limit.'

The commander turned to the two military policemen who were standing behind Bill and demanded to know why the name and serial number they had quoted, were different from those clearly shown on the British soldier's army pay book. The policemen fumbled with their books, until the commander, eventually losing patience with them, shouted, 'Get this guy out of here!' 'With that,' says Bill, 'I was escorted out of the room and told to "Beat it!" I went back to Charminster and heard no more about it.'

During the course of the war, many new weapons and secret tests took place around the country, which also put people in considerable danger. Des Fry recalls the moment when a new menace revealed itself to the population of Weymouth and Portland, in the form of artificial fog. On moonlit nights this foul concoction was produced by machines and canisters, attended at street corners by black American troops. The reason for this smoke screen was to conceal the build up of the invasion forces from enemy aerial reconnaissance. Des explains that it caused problems with anybody suffering from breathing difficulties. He also believes it was responsible for the deaths of some elderly people in the area.

Another way that the men and machines of war affected local people is perfectly illustrated by the villages of Imber on Salisbury Plain, and Tyneham in Dorset. These were deemed necessary for training soldiers in the art of street and other types of fighting, before the invasion. To do this meant removing all the people at very short notice. Sixty years later, the buildings remain empty, as the inhabitants were never allowed to return to their homes. These scars have never healed!

The term 'the fog of war' normally refers to a cover up of some sort, where the civilian population isn't informed of what is going on. One of the best examples of this happened at Slapton Sands in Devon in April 1944, when a training exercise led to the deaths of several hundred American servicemen. However, because the area had been evacuated and nobody was witness to it, the tragedy was kept quiet, and it wasn't until years later that the truth came out.

Dave Ford, who grew up at Underhill on the island of Portland, would often go down to Chesil Beach with his mates, where many Americans,

78 Sherman tank retrieved from the sea off Slapton Sands in Devon, and now on display in the village. Nearby is a plaque: 'Dedicated by the United States of America in honor of the men of the US Army's 1st Engineer Special Brigade, the 4th Infantry Division, and the VII Corps Headquarters: and the US Navy's 11th Amphibious Force who perished in the waters of Lyme Bay during the early hours of April 28, 1944.' (Photo: author)

79 Memorial on Slapton Sands itself which reads: 'This memorial was presented by the United States Army authorities to the people of the South Hams who generously left their homes and their lands to provide a battle practice area for the successful assault in Normandy in June 1944. Their action resulted in the saving of many hundreds of lives and contributed in no small measure to the success of the operation.' The area included the villages of Blackawton, Chillington, East Allington, Sherford, Slapton, Stokenham, Streete and Torcross, together with many outlying farms and houses. (Photo: author)

men and equipment, gathered before the invasion. Following the disaster at Slapton Sands, he was party to the aftermath of this terrible event, even though he didn't realise it at the time. Three of the stricken American landing craft appeared in the cove at Chesil Beach, known to the locals as 'Down Corner'. Here they unloaded dead and wounded. On the day in question Dave was off school. Word quickly spread that the ships were there and, by the time he arrived, a long line of ambulances was parked at Cove Cottages, and he witnessed a procession of stretchers being ferried towards them.

The tragedy at Slapton Sands, although a 'fog of war', has been much written about, documented and researched over the years, but the one thing that sources find it difficult to agree on is the exact number who perished that night: the most commonly quoted figure is 749 dead. But what occurred at Slapton Sands during *Operation Tiger* is only one of several such tragedies to occur during the preparations for D-Day. One rumour tells of dead American troops being secretly buried on wasteland at Poole Quay following a pre-invasion exercise over Hook Sands, a very shallow area just outside the entrance to the harbour. It is suggested that in order not to affect general morale, these casualties were landed and buried secretly as close to the landing point as possible.

Chapter 6

A Time to Relax

Young men the world over need to occupy their spare time as enjoyably as possible, and the wartime Americans in Britain certainly made every effort to enjoy theirs. For those already fighting the war from airbases around England, the ability to relax away from the workplace at the end of the working day, or after returning home from a dangerous mission, was absolutely essential. Free time also proved one of the best ways to meet local people and begin relationships. The same thing applied to the ground forces as they began to build up for D-Day. When there was a lull in training, there were many opportunities to explore the British countryside, and visit local villages and towns to find what was on offer.

In previous chapters we've already touched on the various ways the GIs enjoyed their time off. They were typical young men, who liked music and dancing, going to the movies, or having a few drinks with their friends. Others liked to spend their time helping in the community, and taking part in local clubs and activities. It was at this point that the Americans were most visible to the British public, and at this point they were able to show both the very best, and the very worst, aspects of their characters.

Many things to see and do

Although the Americans had an abundance of vehicles for use during furloughs, in the 1940s with petrol rationing, the preferred mode of transport in rural Britain was the bicycle.

At Dereham in Norfolk, Tony Blades recalls how the thirst for English bicycles among the airmen at Shipdham led to their being disadvantaged. 'There were some English people who didn't like the Americans,' he explains, 'mainly I think because of their popularity with English girls, and because they had money, smart uniforms, and an attractive accent. So they took advantage of them. The Americans had no off duty transport to town, which was about four miles away, so they were keen to buy bikes and a number of men and boys took advantage of this.'

These individuals would comb through dumps, scrap-heaps, hedges, and anywhere else they could pick up old bits of bikes, which they would then transform into what were literally 'bone-shakers' which they sold to the Yanks at extortionate prices. Some of them were hardly road worthy.

80   Military Policemen, who were camped near Upton Lovell, Wiltshire, in 1943 – with a haul of trout. This photo came to light when Barbara Saunt was setting up an exhibition for the Millennium celebrations at the nearby village of Corton. It was donated by Mr David Fostick, whose mother had it for many years, and told him that the soldier in the picture not wearing a hat was Corporal Dippary, who had been a regular visitor to her family home. The river Wylye was dredged during the war to make it too deep for tanks to cross, in case of invasion from the south coast. It must also have made it ideal for fishing? (Photo: courtesy of Mrs V. Mulholland)

81   303rd airmen enjoying a game of baseball, which seems to have been a standard form of relaxation for off-duty GIs. (Photo: courtesy of 303rd Bomb Group Association/ George T. Mackin)

82   Bill Overley, an American serviceman in Cheltenham, cycles around Pittville Park where there was a tented camp in front of the Pump Room. (Photo: courtesy of Jennifer Mason)

However, the Americans had the last laugh as, when the war ended and they were about to leave, Tony and his friends went over to Shipdham looking for freebies. 'I can still see this pile of bikes,' he explains, 'hundreds of them! There must have been at least 500. Being cheeky youngsters we asked if we could have one each. The reply was, "No, we paid you English good money for these goddam bikes, stick around and you will see what we are going to do with them." We did stick around, to see one of their mighty tracked vehicles crush the lot. We deserved that – they had gotten wise to us.'

In a letter home, cartoonist and fighter pilot George Rarey said of this mode of transport: 'They have issued us English bicycles – they are fine vehicles and we have a lot of fun riding in formation, etc. They will never, however, take the place of the airplane – the main drawback being that they are too dangerous.'

Most English villages had a pub, and towns had many, all of which proved magnets for the Americans and their money. Bryan Potter was around 12 years old and living in Southgate Street, Bury St Edmunds when the Rougham airbase was used by the Americans. At every opportunity, and particularly between bombing missions, the airmen would descend on Bury to socialise. Bryan recalls:

> I well remember one extremely young airman called Bobby, who befriended our family during rousing evenings in the former *Coach & Horses* pub. Just a week after he had gifted my brother and I beautiful bone-handled pocketknives I detected a depression in the family. Later I was reluctantly informed that he had been shot down over Berlin. There was great sadness at the thought of his death. Although we later learned he had been taken prisoner.

During the war years Walter Perry was living at Clare in Suffolk, where his parents kept a small county pub about three miles from the base at Ridgewell. Several Americans regularly visited the pub

83   George Rarey wrote of English bicycles: 'They will never, however, take the place of the airplane – the main drawback being that they are too dangerous.' (Illustration: courtesy of Linda Rarey and the EAA Museum)

and the family got to know them well. These Americans found it hard to comprehend not having their beer chilled, but served at cellar temperature. 'A favourite drink of the time,' he states, 'was half a pint of bitter topped up with a small IPA bottled beer, this was known as Eno's; or conversely mild beer topped with a small Burton ale which was known as Nut and Bolt. The Americans thought this somewhat quaint, but embraced the taproom beer names very quickly.'

The identity of one particular visitor to *The Carpenters Arms* in St Mary's, Chalford, in Gloucestershire, remains a mystery, although he might have been someone quite famous. At the time the pub was run by the parents of John Astridge, who was himself away serving with the Royal Navy. One evening at about 7p.m. a coloured American came into the pub for a drink. There were no other people in the bar at the time, so he had one drink and then left. While departing he called, 'Thanks Mac, I've left you a present on the mantel shelf'. The landlady replied with her thanks and went into the taproom, where on the mantelpiece there were two oranges and a photo. The photo was the portrait of a black sergeant in uniform, and on the back were scribbled the words, 'Staff Sgt. Joe Louis, 10.6.1944, somewhere in England'.

'Was it Joe Louis?' asks John Astridge, 'and why did he cross out his first signature? We shall never know.' Indeed, looking at the back of the photograph, which Mr Astridge still has, the first signature is mysteriously crossed out, but then followed by the same inscription, 'Joe Louis'.

At the time Joe Louis (Barrow) was the World Heavyweight Boxing champion, a title he held from 1937 to 1949. He joined the Army in 1942 as an athletic instructor, and in the photograph the subject wears a whistle on his uniform, a clear indication that he was. In March 1944 he went overseas, taking part in exhibition fights and talks, entertaining more than 2,000,000 soldiers. For his incalculable contribution to the general morale of these troops he was awarded the Legion of Merit, and today local people still tell legendary accounts of Joe Louis fighting all over the West Country from Chilcompton in Somerset, to Torquay in Devon.

The family of Bernard Peters lived beside River Walk in Truro, where his father had a barber's shop. On many evenings, he can recall American friends drying off in their saloon, having fallen in

84   A GI poses with English bicycles outside a hut at Molesworth. (Photo: courtesy of 303rd Bomb Group Association)

85 These Ameri-
cans are out for
a summer ride
in their best
uniforms, no
doubt heading for
the nearest pub.
(Photo: courtesy
of 303rd Bomb
Group Association)

the harbour. At the time the house was opposite a fish and chip shop. It was very dark in the evenings, with the blackout in operation. There were no streetlights and such vehicles as there were had special visors on their headlamps. To go into the chip shop, a curtain had to be pulled aside for a brief moment. The pubs called 'Time' at 10 o'clock and the GIs would stagger out and queue up for fish and chips.

'Whilst waiting in the queue,' Bernard recalls, 'having had several pints of beer, they would need to have a pee. So they would come across the road and go down the tide slipway to stand on the river bank which was approximately 18 foot above the water at low tide.' From their house the whole family could hear the peeing at high tide. They could also hear when an unsteady American, slipped down the muddy sloping bank, which had no railings, and fell in the water. 'We would hear the splash or a shout,' he recalls, 'and Dad would say, "Another

86   John B. Thomas (on right) with friends enjoying the English countryside on their American Army motorcycles. (Photo: courtesy of Jane Smith)

87 GIs enjoying a pint of English ale at their bar in Molesworth. (Photo: courtesy of Mark Forlow)

silly bugger fallen in." That is how more than once they would be in Dad's saloon with Mum drying their clothing by the stove, and them towelling themselves.'

Hazel Green lived in Appleshaw in Hampshire, close to the large camp at Tidworth on the edge of Salisbury Plain. The village had three pubs and when beer was available the Yanks would drink happily with the locals. She occasionally played the piano in one of the pubs, and says that the favourite song with the GIs was, *Don't sit under the apple tree with anyone else but me.* Hazel would regularly go into

88 George Rarey's depiction of Yanks and locals enjoying a drink in a village pub. (Illustration: courtesy of Linda Rarey and the EAA Museum)

the pub, put her music upon the piano, and take requests from the gathered crowd. Some of the other popular songs she remembers being asked to play included *Moonlight Serenade*; *Paper Moon*; and *Blue birds over the white cliffs of Dover.*

One thing that endeared many Americans to the hearts of local people was their willingness to join in with the community. Rosemary Allen met some Americans who made a great impression on her, as a group of them would attend Sunday services at the Baptist chapel in Swaffham, where her own family worshipped. The ladies of the church would invite the airmen to tea and, once or twice, a few would grace their own home. 'Goodness knows what mother fed them on out of our meagre rations,' ponders Rosemary, 'but she was always very good at making meals out of very little. I think the church was trying to make them feel welcome and part of the community.'

89 The photograph which was left on the mantelpiece at *The Carpenters Arms*, St Mary's Chalford. The inscription on the back reads 'Staff Sgt Joe Louis 10.6.1944, somewhere in England.' (Photo: courtesy of John Astridge)

The church was a common and unifying bond for many Americans and local people. Vera Bassett was a teenager in Norwich at the time and a regular member of the Rosebery Road Methodist Church, which had an extremely happy and thriving youth club. Several American airmen stationed at St Faiths became regular attendees of both church and club and the local people readily welcomed them into their society. This situation led to several long-lasting friendships.

Vera herself became particularly friendly with a young officer called Lieutenant Henry Fraysier, who sang as a tenor in the church choir, so they spent many happy times together. During the years since the end of the war, not only have Henry and his wife visited Vera and her husband, but so have his brother and son, keeping close ties with the people and location of his service.

The following is an extract from the Rosebery Road Methodist Church Youth Club diary, which provides us with contemporary evidence of how American servicemen were only too willing to become involved with the local communities.

March 1st 1944: Throughout the winter of 1944, the need for some form of heating in the large schoolroom was extremely apparent. Owing to the fuel shortage it was impossible to use the original heating system.

90 This George Rarey cartoon illustrates some of the delights that GIs might experience on a furlough in London. (Illustration: courtesy of Linda Rarey and the EAA Museum)

So a plan was devised by our American friend Dana Cook, for installing a slow combustion stove fitted with an electric fan. The proceeds of our Christmas Pantomime in 1944 met the cost of this innovation and permission was then given by the trustees, for the installation. Dana, with his friend Glenn, began working on the stove on March 1st and the results of their labours are greatly appreciated in the winter months by all Badminton and Table tennis players.

A subsequent entry in the diary dated later in the same month, mentions Don Scranton, who was another of the American servicemen that attended the Rosebery Road Methodist Church. The entry tells of a trip to Coltishall, which is roughly ten or eleven miles from the centre of Norwich. We assume their transport on this occasion, was bicycles.

March 30th 1944: On Good Friday morning a large group of us rode out to Coltishall to a service at our Methodist Church there. We had a splendid service in which some of us took part, Sheila Gardner singing and Don Scranton reading the lesson. In spite of a terrific biting head wind on our return journey we have a happy snap taken of this outing to show you we were not dismayed. This is just one of the many excursions we make to country churches.

Glenn Hynick, Don Scranton and Henry Fraysier were all based at Horsham St Faith during their stay in East Anglia, which was the headquarters of 96th Combat Wing, USAAF, and the airfield at which the B-24s of 458th Bomb Group were based.

Allan Thomas was brought up in Helston in Cornwall and was the youngest of five children. As a family they were all members of a little Methodist church in Meneage Street, where his mother and father were big helpers. Allan was 15 when the Americans came and on Friday nights he used to go to the youth club. One Friday night on his way to the club, he stopped to talk to a couple of American soldiers and invited them to come to chapel on the Sunday, which they did. One was called Al and the other Will. His mother and father invited them home for supper, after which they became regular visitors to the house. Allan particularly palled up with Will and wrote to his mother in America. Allan's own mother and sister used to help in the 'Donut Dugout', and they would bring home some of the doughnuts, which he loved. 'I have never tasted any other doughnuts as good', he says.

They got to know other soldiers as well, who would also come to the house, particularly if they were musical, as the Thomas's were a musical family. Will suggested that he and Allan should go to the photographer to have a photograph taken of them together, which he sent home to his mother. After the Americans left Helston for the D-Day landings, they lost touch with each other until 1988, when Will's mother died. Going through her effects Will discovered the letters that Allan had written to her. He decided to contact Allan and wrote to the address in Helston, at which he had been welcomed all those years ago. By now Allan had moved to Bodmin, but the letter was luckily forwarded. As a result of this, Will returned to England and the Normandy beaches with

91 Outside Rosebery Road Methodist Church, Norwich. The young man directly under the word 'Rosebery' on the sign is Don Scranton, and next to him in uniform is Glenn Hynick. Both were stationed at Horsham St Faith, and regularly attended church services and youth club meetings. The young lady to the right of Don is youth club member Vera Bassett (née Thompson) and also in the photo, bottom left, are the Reverend George and Mrs Strangroom, who ran the youth club. (Photo: courtesy of Vera Bassett)

92 Will Gamble and Allan Thomas, taken in Helston, Cornwall. Will went to Normandy on D-Day, but 45 years later retraced Allan after finding a letter from him in his late mother's personal effects. (Photo: courtesy of Allan Thomas)

his wife, to revisit all the places at which he had served. In turn, Allan and his wife went to Will's home in Sacramento, where they met his daughter, who kindly sent them details of her father's funeral service when he passed away in 2004.

MOVIES, MUSIC AND DANCING

In Britain, at the time of the Second World War, many people associated America with movies, music, and dancing. Hollywood in particular was a factory for manufacturing entertainment to the world. So when the Americans came to England, music, dancing and films would always feature in their off-duty activities.

Once a week the US troops laid on a film show at the village school in Broadstone, in Dorset. Roy Stevens remembers seeing one film which featured the Andrews Sisters, in which they sang the song *Sentimental Journey.* He was so taken with them that he remembered them in his prayers that night.

In some places, if the Americans didn't put on their own film shows, they were quite happy to accompany local children to the nearest cinema. John Owen has happy memories of going to the cinema in Warrington, Lancashire, because if you waited outside for an American to happen along he would invariably pay for your ticket and give you chewing gum. He might also, if you were very lucky, give you 'unheard of chocolate marshmallows'.

Karen Holyoake was one of five sisters whose ages ranged from seven to 13, who were each given 6d. to go to the local cinema every Saturday afternoon. Once in 1944, after their one-and-a-half-mile walk, they arrived only to discover that one of the sisters had lost her money. This was a disaster, because it meant that none of them could go in and watch *Tarzan of the Apes*, or whatever exciting film was showing.

Karen spotted two American soldiers walking down the road and, plucking up courage, approached them with her tale of woe. The Americans happily gave them the 6d. and some chewing gum, which she says they tried to refuse, but the Yanks insisted. The girls asked for their address in order to return their money, but they wouldn't hear of it, saying they were 'pleased and delighted to help five such lovely English girls'.

Karen explains that when they got home they didn't dare tell their mother that they had asked strangers for money. She would have been very angry, and would no doubt have banned their next week's outing. Quite probably, she would also have given them all a good spanking.

In Oxford, there was the famous Churchill Hospital, where many wounded GIs were nursed back to health. Gordon Tunnicliffe lived on an estate, which he describes as being, 'only a stone's throw from the hospital entrance'. At 18 he was called up into the British Army, spending part of his service in the Sudan, but he recalls befriending several Americans while they were there, and can even recall them playing American football matches on the rugby ground at Oxford University. But perhaps his most interesting recollection is of the open-air concert given at the hospital by the Glenn Miller band.

Glenn Miller's band, which had been formed in America from the top musicians of the day, came to Europe to entertain the troops, with Miller himself given the rank of major. When the band performed at the Churchill, Gordon had the privilege of watching the show from the lawns. This was around June/July 1944, he notes, and was put on to entertain injured soldiers evacuated from France. So obviously D-Day had already taken place. To back his story up, Gordon has two faded but interesting photographs of the band in action.

93 A Christmas dance being held at the American Red Cross Club in Newbury, Berkshire, where the mother of Wendy Rennison worked during the war. Note the three flags draped at the back of the hall: Union Jack, Stars and Stripes, and Red Cross. (Photo: courtesy of Wendy Rennison)

For Betty Traves, a love of dancing in the American style led to many friendships. She was working in a large department store in Bournemouth, while at the same time the Yanks were billeted in most of the large hotels on the West Cliff, all of which had been commandeered for their use. They used to have lots of dances and the shop girls were invited to all of them.

'We had some super times,' Betty recalls, 'and if any of them misbehaved our managing director would take it up with their commanding officer, and they were reprimanded! If one of our girls had that special date, there was a little black dress, that did the rounds quite often; I cannot remember now whose it was. We also got invited to the camps at Blandford and Bovington. They would come and fetch us, and we were taken in one of those awful large army trucks and brought home again after the dance holding on for dear life as they swayed all over the place down those very narrow lanes. But we loved going, as the dances were such fun, with the big band playing all the Glenn Miller arrangements. Also on a warm sunny evening we were able to walk around the camp, with that special someone. By this time I had met a special Yank, but he was called to go overseas, and I never heard from him again.'

Betty notes that regular dances took place at the *Hotel Miramar* and the church hall at Christchurch; some were even held on Sunday afternoons. 'I would be anywhere that there was a jive going on,' she admits.

Beryl Reeser also remembers Bournemouth at the time, saying that, 'Even though it was wartime, it was a fun time for single girls'. Most of the American units in the area had their own bands and she can remember dancing on the cliffs on a Sunday afternoon. The pavilion in Bournemouth was also a big attraction where various activities

94 A faded but rare snapshot of the Glenn Miller band, performing in front of wounded American soldiers at the Churchill Hospital in Oxford, in June/July 1944. Gordon Tunnicliffe, who was in the audience, believes that the man in officer's uniform at the back of the front group is Miller himself. (Photo: courtesy of Gordon Tunnicliffe)

95 The Rhythm Pilots, the 303rd BG(H) Dance Band, pictured in March 1945. (Photo: courtesy of 303rd Bomb Group Association/George T. Mackin)

were held. Additionally, she can remember an American band regularly playing on the patio of the *Hotel Miramar*. Beryl and her girlfriend would walk to the tea dances there as often as they could.

As a teenager at the time, Mrs J. Bryant was working at the Van Heusen factory in Taunton on war work, and remembers weekend dances at the American camps at Musgrove Hospital and Dunkeswell airfield. The council offices, she recalls, became a club that the Yanks would have to sign girls into. Then there was the County Ballroom, which was very popular with town girls, because it didn't necessitate an uncomfortable journey in the back of a truck to get there. 'If a Yank was getting married,' she says, 'they would send trucks into Taunton to pick up girls for dancing partners for the guests. The food was out of this world. In fact, I think my friends and I spent a lot of time in the kitchen.'

In London, some girls volunteered to become dance hostesses, when the Stage Door Canteen was opened in Piccadilly. One such girl was Gwen Ghijben, who worked in an insurance office in St James's Street. Although many girls from her office were called up for various forms of service, some were not, and Gwen's parents didn't wish her to volunteer. Instead she did a little charity work for the YMCA but also went dancing at Covent Garden once a week, which was then a dance hall where the Ivy Benson Band played throughout the war. Here she met soldiers from many nations, and when the Americans entered the war she found them 'pleasant and perfect gentlemen'.

Gwen noticed an advertisement in the *Evening News* asking for girls to become hostesses for the opening of the Stage Door Canteen, where servicemen from many nations could be entertained while in the capital. Gwen and a few of her friends applied and were accepted. The

96   An earlier photograph of the Rhythm Pilots, this time dated 22 April 1943. (Photo: courtesy of 303rd Bomb Group Association/George T. Mackin)

hostesses were formed into groups of 20, each under the charge of an older lady. There were probably around 700 recruited in total, working every evening, in two shifts. The scheme was under the direction of Mrs Leigh-Lye, whose late husband Colonel Leigh-Lye had held a responsible post in the Ministry of Pensions. She interviewed and selected girls that were well educated, were of irreproachable character, and had social gifts that enabled them to be a success. The ability to speak foreign languages was also an advantage.

Gwen and her friends were given Saturday evenings, provided with sashes to wear, and instructed never to refuse to dance with anyone that asked them. Entertainers also appeared at the club, and on Gwen's evening it was the turn of Bea Lillie. During this part of the proceedings everyone sat on the floor and she says, 'The Americans loved it. After the war the venue was changed to Rainbow Corner, Shaftesbury Avenue.' She met many Americans in this role, while another highlight from her wartime memories of London was when the Yanks took over the Palladium for a Special American Show.

For young ladies working in London throughout the Second World War dancing became an important part of their lives. Mrs M. Borman was a teenager working as a secretary in Piccadilly Circus, so after work she would meet up with her friends and regularly visit dance halls, such as the Lyceum in the Strand, or the Covent Garden Opera House, both of which were used to hold dances during the war. Here they met numerous GIs on leave from their various units, and she describes London as being a magnet for these soldiers, sailors and airmen. 'Dances were a popular means of entertainment in those dark days,' she admits, 'enabling us to forget our troubles for a few hours while listening and dancing to the music of the big bands of the day.'

Some of these young men made repeated visits to the capital and she was able to take a few of them home to meet the family, finding them very generous with their gifts of chocolates and nylon stockings for the ladies of the house, and cigarettes for her father. She describes them as being full of charisma, with good manners, always polite and well presented. Being financially better off than British soldiers on leave in the city, they always bought the best seats in the house when they went to the theatre or cinema, a situation which must surely have ruffled a few native feathers.

But wherever American soldiers were based, you could guarantee that dances would shortly follow, even in small rural towns and villages. It must have been quite early in 1943, after American Army engineers had arrived in the Dorset town of Beaminster, that they posted a notice on the window of a requisitioned shop in the town square: 'Dance will he held Tonite in the Public Hall'. This hall had been used as the mess hall by the British Army who had recently moved out, and it had a temporary cookhouse alongside it. Everyone was invited and Jim Timoney's mother, who worked during the evenings in the fish and chip shop, was asked to provide tin baths full of chips, which were placed on the dance floor for all to consume. Beer, at that time still available, was brought into the hall in barrels and a good time was had by all.

From the village of Appleshaw in Hampshire, Hazel Green remembers going with her friends to the Cadre Club in Tidworth for dances. She too recalls that they were picked up by American trucks, and later dropped off home again to make sure they were safe. 'The American soldiers respected the villagers and the young girls,' she says. 'They were always very polite and never overstepped their boundaries.'

Also at Tidworth, where Olive Martin both lived and helped out in the Red Cross club, there was a loudspeaker system throughout the barrack area, which broadcast music all day long to the soldiers in camp. This played the recorded music of Glenn Miller, the big bands, and of course all the popular vocalists of the era, such as Bing Crosby, Frank Sinatra, and Ella Fitzgerald. Every evening around five o'clock the American national anthem would be played and everything and everyone came to a standstill. During the summer evenings an American Army band played on a football field near Olive's house and the troops would march to the music. She particularly remembers the *St Louis Blues March*. These were difficult and worrying times, but the American Army did their best to keep up the morale of their troops. Broadcasting music was one way of doing this.

And at Devizes in Wiltshire, Bill Underwood remembers Christmas 1943, when the men of the 4th Armored Division descended on the town. There were so many Americans in Sheep Street, that the place resembled the 'Wild West', he thought. Vehicles were parked all along the street, and soldiers were shouting, swearing, singing and fighting. 'I was in bed trying to get some sleep,' he recalls, 'when I heard Miss Bayley's voice. "Would you mind being quiet", she said, "my mother's dying." Suddenly it all went quiet as a respectful hush fell over the town. Then a lone soldier started singing *Silent Night* and everyone gradually joined in. Soon the street was filled with a sound that contrasted so dramatically with the shouted obscenities and cursing that had been hushed by the lady's plea.'

Bill Underwood goes on to point out that the lady who was so gravely ill did not in fact pass away until after D-Day. It is therefore

97 The girls: Betty Traves, on the left, with her friends Christine and Marjorie, during a five-day trip to Derby where they met up with their American friends, Bill, Wally and Shorty. Betty and her best friend Christine worked at a departmental store in Bournemouth, and loved dancing with the Americans. (Photo: courtesy of Betty Traves)

98 The boys: Bill, Wally and Shorty, pictured during their five-day visit to Derby, to meet Betty, Marjorie, and Christine. Betty says that Wally was quite keen on her, but she didn't fancy him. Bill married Marjorie in 1945. (Photo: courtesy of Betty Traves)

very probable that many of the boys who sang to her so poignantly that night died before she did.

Violent Times

Britain in the 1940s was still relatively law-abiding and, even though we had been at war for several years, violence on the streets was a thing associated more with American movies. In reality, as the fights between northerners and southerners, and whites and blacks, have already indicated, America was indeed a more volatile and violent place than the rural towns and villages of East Anglia and the West Country that were about to be invaded.

Many of the black servicemen stationed at Eye in Suffolk would go into Ipswich to socialise and visit the public houses and, although the British people were quite ready to mix with them, the white GIs were not. This not only led to many fights, usually over local women, but (as previously noted) to the adoption of a form of segregation. On the part of the British, this segregation wasn't induced by racism, but by the need to keep order on the streets. Ipswich effectively became a divided city. This meant that certain pubs, such as the *White Horse* and the *Running Buck*, were out of bounds to the black soldiers. However, there were still many savage and bloody battles between the two sides, and stabbings were fairly common.

David Hay who lived on a farm near Andover during the war recalls how fights between black and white Americans were common in the pubs in the area, until one coloured American was knifed and died in a public house in Kingsclere. After this the two racial groups had to have alternate nights.

In the 1940s, Roy Mellor was a schoolboy living in the station sergeant's flat at the police station in Bury St Edmunds, where his father Charles Mellor was station sergeant. On arrival in the town, the American military police set up a small office inside an unused shop that was located on the Cornhill. From all the bases located in the area, many servicemen would come in to Bury during the evenings, to drink, dance, and let off steam.

Not far from the MP's office, a local news-vendor known as Sam had a pitch, and Roy remembers vividly an incident when an American serviceman got into trouble one night and evidently Sam had been involved. The serviceman hi-jacked a Jeep containing some of his compatriots and drove to the office, where he demanded to be taken to Sam's address. He produced a colt 45 pistol and fired a shot at one of the MPs, which parted his hair down the middle. Forcing the policeman into the Jeep at gunpoint, the soldier then demanded to be taken to see Sam. The officer drove around for a while deciding what to do, and eventually ferried his armed passenger to the police station in St

99   Invitation to the 303rd's 2nd Birthday Party, 3 February 1944. (Photo: courtesy of 303rd Bomb Group Association)

100   Invitation to a dance on 10 February 1945. (Photo: courtesy of 303rd Bomb Group Association/ Blanche (Barnes) Gangwere)

John's Street, pretending it to be the home of his intended victim. Their knock at the door was answered by a British bobby, which visibly shook the American, who, incensed by this act of treachery, pulled out a hand grenade and put it in his mouth, threatening to pull out the pin. Roy Mellor's father, becoming aware of the commotion, appeared and diffused the situation by bravely snatching the hand grenade from the man's mouth. Following this, the man was quickly overpowered and, when he was searched later, two further hand grenades were found concealed on his person.

Mary Singleton was a student nurse at the Bristol Royal Infirmary and she remembers an incident down at the Horsefair when a white GI, wanted by an MP for questioning, jumped on to a bus. The driver was ordered to

101   Sergeant Mellor of the Bury St Edmunds Police Force, who had an encounter with a violent GI. (Photo: courtesy of Roy Mellor)

stop, but he didn't take orders from a Yank, so drove on. The MP shot into the crowded bus and got his man. By the time Mary got back to the hospital the man was in casualty, with four or five doctors around him, but they were unable to save him. 'I wonder what he had done?', she asks.

Similarly, David Dodge remembers an incident at Warminster in Wiltshire, where there was a short-cut from the American Army barracks to the town, through an area called Copheap. 'One day,' he says, 'a prisoner had escaped from the guardroom in the camp, and was thought to be hiding in the Copheap trees. A party of armed soldiers was sent to recapture him. At the same time, a small group of off-duty soldiers was using the short-cut into town. One of them stopped to tie his shoelace, while the others continued along the path. When he started to run to catch them up, one of the search party mistook him for the escapee, fired his rifle and killed him.'

In rural England in the early 1940s, murder was certainly a rare occurrence. It was therefore little wonder that the sleepy inhabitants of Essex were shocked by the brutal killing of 28-year-old Harry Hailstone in December 1943. Alan Shillum, the news editor of the *Community News* which covers an area along the River Blackwater from Maldon to West Mersea, has done much research into this case, which is still today cloaked with mystery.

To set the scene, there were several US bases in the area, including one at Birch, outside Tiptree, which was a bomber base and home of the 410th Bomb Group, 9th USAAF, which flew A-20 Havocs. Two black servicemen from Birch who were members of the 356th Engineer Regiment were convicted of Harry's murder, but Alan still wonders about the truth. He explains that the spot where the murder took place has since changed beyond all recognition, and even Harry's own ghost would find it difficult to locate the exact spot.

'Somewhere in the vicinity of vanished Birch Rectory,' he writes, 'and the lane to Hardy's Green, Harry, a likeable and harmless cab driver, was robbed and strangled. Stand there of an evening today, with a westerly rustling the trees, wait for a lull in the roar of traffic and listen. You might, if your imagination's good, just hear on the breeze a sound like the harmony of a swing band saxophone section. Of course, it's just a trick of the wind sighing across the lonely fields between Messing and Birch Green, but when I heard it, as I combed the lanes on an autumn evening, it conjured up the time when the strains of jazz were commonplace in this bit of Essex countryside. For in the grim war years between 1942 and 1945, American troops lived and worked here – most evenings playing their music on 78rpm gramophones and the camp PA system.'

On the day that Harry Hailstone died, the area buzzed with activity as engineer battalions laid down concrete runways and hard standings for the bomber base. Many of these troops were Afro-Americans and, although most people in this rural backwater had never seen a black man before, Alan explains that 'there was an affinity with these homesick lads torn from the rural deep South'.

When these troops put on a tea for scores of local children, giving up their rations to do so, and giving each child a present, the *Essex Chronicle* printed the headline, 'The Darkies give a party.' Today this might seem offensive, but put into the context of 60 years ago it was meant as an affectionate 'Thank you.'

Harry's abandoned cab was discovered by a police constable while on patrol in Haynes Green Lane. There were signs of a struggle, such as blood on the rear seat and damaged upholstery. He also found papers, some gloves and an empty wallet, all of which suggested foul play. The police mounted a search and two days later Harry's body was found in the grounds of Birch Rectory. Several clues within the car and at the murder scene led to the arrest of two American soldiers

102   Mary Singleton was a student nurse at the Bristol Royal Infirmary. She recalls an incident when an American MP shot a GI on a city bus. The man later died in casualty. This was her official photo taken at the BRI. (Photo: courtesy of Mary Singleton)

103 1199th Military Police Company on parade at Molesworth, 30 March 1944. Note the British telephone box in background. (Photo: courtesy of 303rd Bomb Group Association/Paul O Harmon)

based at Birch airfield, 22-year-old George E. Fowler and 21-year-old J.C. Leatherberry.

Under questioning Fowler told the police that he and his friend had gone to London that night drinking with a party of GIs. On the train journey back, Leatherberry made the suggestion that they hire a cab from Colchester train station to take them back to the camp and rob the driver. Fowler claimed not to agree with the plan, but did admit to getting into Hailstone's cab.

Fowler went on to describe what happened when he asked the driver to stop on the way to the camp, in order to relieve himself. As he got out of the taxi, he heard Leatherberry shout, and turning back saw the man standing up in the back of the vehicle, holding the driver with his left hand and punching him with the right. The cab driver went limp and Leatherberry dragged him on to the back seat, saying, 'We've got to stick together'. Fowler agreed to help his friend dispose of the body, which they pushed under the fence of the Rectory on the other side of the road. According to Fowler's testimony, Leatherberry drove the taxi to Maldon, hoping to catch a train back to London, but, on finding that the last train had already gone, he drove back towards Birch, dumping the taxi near the camp.

Allan Shillum explains that, 'Leatherberry strenuously denied he was involved because, he said, he was in London on the night of the murder, but he and Fowler were held in Colchester police station for fingernail scrapings to be taken. There was blood under all of Leatherberry's nails, but only one of Fowler's. Leatherberry stuck to his story, however, even under intensive questioning, but was charged with murder along with Fowler on December 14 and handed over to the US military.'

The court-martials of both men took place at Ipswich Town Hall at the same time but in different rooms. Both pleading innocent, Fowler's trial lasted 12 hours and Leatherberry's 14 hours. Fowler even gave evidence against his friend, and although Leatherberry's defence produced two witnesses supporting his claim of being in London at the time of the crime, he was found guilty and sentenced to death. Fowler on the other hand, although also found guilty, had so impressed the court that he was given a sentence of life imprisonment with hard labour in a US penitentiary.

Leatherberry was executed on 16 May 1944 at Shepton Mallet prison. Standing on the gallows platform and after the charges and sentence had been read out, he was asked if he had anything to say and replied, 'I want to thank the guys for everything as they were so nice to me, the guards and everything.' To the chaplain he said, 'Sir, I want to thank you for being so nice to me and for everything you have done for me.'

'Frustratingly for those involved,' concludes Alan Shillum, 'Leatherberry went to his grave without admitting guilt. Ever since then, the question has been asked, "Did he kill Harry Hailstone – or did someone else get away with murder?" If so, who? Fowler was released from jail in 1960 after serving just 16 years of his "life" sentence. As far as is known he never changed the story he told the court.'

Some of the worst racial violence to take place in England during the Second World War happened on 24 June 1943, when black soldiers stationed at Bamber Bridge in Lancashire, headquarters of the 1511th Quartermaster Truck Regiment, stormed into the town looking for white MPs, after several of their comrades had been mistreated earlier on leaving the pub. The situation resulted in a pitched battle in the street, in which several black soldiers were shot, one of whom died from his wounds several days later.

A similar riot took place at Launceston in Cornwall on 26 September 1943, when black soldiers who had newly arrived in the area were incensed by the fact that they were not permitted to drink in the same part of the pub as white GIs. A group of soldiers later returned to the town armed with Tommy guns, rifles and bayonets, shooting and seriously wounding two MPs.

Many other parts of the country also witnessed scenes of racial tension, including Leicester, where white paratroopers of the 82nd Airborne Division had taunted black soldiers because they had observed them escorting white women to the local pubs and dances. This situation ended with the death of an Airborne Division MP. Similarly, Bristol experienced numerous racially motivated fights.

But perhaps one of the saddest incidents of all is the one remembered by David Hay at Kingsclere in Berkshire, which happened because men of the all-black 3247 Quartermaster Service Company were told to leave the pub, the *Bolton Arms*, by MPs, because they didn't have the necessary passes. One of the soldiers subsequently claimed that an MP had cocked a rifle at him. Later that evening, a number of black soldiers returned to the village, scouring several pubs in search of the policemen. The resulting gun battle left three people dead: one of the black GIs,

104 The Military Police Company at Molesworth had personnel carriers, Jeeps, and this solitary motorcycle. (Photo: courtesy of 303rd Bomb Group Association/Paul O Harmon)

who had been shot in the head; one of the MPs, shot through the heart; and Mrs Rose Napper, the wife of the landlord of *The Crown Inn*. Most of those involved were found guilty of murder, riotous assembly and being absent without leave, for which they received life sentences with hard labour. But the strangest thing about this particular incident was the fact that the murdered MP was himself black.

CHAPTER 7

Guys and Dolls

The common perception of American soldiers in Britain during the Second World War adheres to the cliché that they were 'oversexed, over paid, and over here'. They were predatory animals, always prowling for young susceptible English girls. Of course there are two sides to every story, and if one or two people in a group seem loud, over-confident, and out for a good time, we tend to overlook the many more shy, retiring, lonely souls that stayed in their billets at night writing letters home to their mothers. I think it's also fair to say, that the label in question was often given tongue in cheek.

However, relationships between wartime Yanks and English girls remains a controversial topic even today and still rankles with some people, as it unquestionably did devastate lives. In this chapter there are examples from both camps, although the vast majority of people remember the Americans as being 'decent young men'. If a gentleman is better paid, better dressed, and seems to generate a sense of glamour, it's inevitable that he will attract attention. The same principle applies today, although in wartime Britain, with the male population of the country largely away at war, the American visitors seemed to offer it all.

Decent young men

With regard to their attitude towards British women during the war, the Americans have always received a lot of bad publicity, but Hilda Willsone remembers all those with whom she associated to be well behaved and says, 'I have nothing but happy memories of them'.

In 1942 Hilda was 18 and in the ATS. Her first posting after training was to Alderbury near Salisbury from July until November, where an American unit occupied Longford Castle. When they had dances, they would send a truck to the ATS billet to take any girls who wished to attend. She fell in love with one GI she reveals, 'but only went out with him for a couple of weeks before they were all moved out, so didn't get to know him except that he came from Pennsylvania. As a souvenir he autographed his flashlight and gave it to me. I still have it.'

A year later, after being posted to Shrewsbury, she came across many more Americans. Here too they would transport the girls to their dances, and she remembers joining them in a building at the Wrekin, the renowned beauty sport of which Bob Powell told us earlier. She spent a year in Shrewsbury, and got to know a few of the men. Her

105 486th Bomb Group members out on the town in London, with young ladies and bandleader Artie Shaw (left). (Photo: copyright 486th Bomb Group Association)

experience was that they often just wanted someone to talk to about their folks back home. 'They were well aware of the shortages we were having,' she points out, 'and I remember being taken into the kitchen and invited to help myself to any food and fruit. My thanks were all that he wanted.'

In 1942 aged 23, Margaret Chesterton worked in the AID (Aeronautical Inspection Directorate) in Westland Aircraft, Yeovil. Several girls including herself used to work in the evenings in the Red Cross Centre, under the charge of ladies from the American Red Cross, and the men would come in and ask locals for various information, or to help them write letters. Margaret admits that this resulted in many dates to go to the pictures with the men, all of whom she found to be 'very well-mannered and pleasant'.

'Only one was a bit too much,' she reveals. 'He was in the hospital with trench foot, which made my work mates roar with laughter when they heard of it. He was "all hands" in the pictures, and my friends used to laugh and tell me they saw me come up for air every so often! He told me he wanted to have a nice English girl to take home with him – not me, I told him, and when I saw him in town later, he came up to tell me he had found one. He seemed to me to be a bit simple.'

Sometimes at night Margaret would make her way home in the blackout all on her own through the streets of Yeovil. At that time she explains, nobody thought twice about walking alone in the dark, as attacks on women were never heard of. On one occasion she became aware of footsteps following her, and admits to becoming slightly worried. Before long the person following her caught her up and a voice said, 'Please miss, can I walk with you?' Margaret explained that she only had a short way to go, up Hendford Hill, but the American begged, 'Please let me come with you, I am so lonely'. So she agreed, and the man walked along beside her and chatted for a while.

'He was called Louis,' Margaret remembers, 'and came from Brooklyn. I can't remember his other name. He said he was at Houndstone Camp, where most of them were in the hospital, and that tomorrow he was going back "over there." He said he was a parachutist, and plain scared. He'd seen some action, and was afraid he was going to be killed. I tried to cheer him up, and he asked if he could call on me in the morning to say goodbye. We got to my digs and he left, saying he would see me in the morning. I didn't give it another thought, as I expected it to be just polite talk, but at six o'clock in the morning my landlord called to me to say there was a Yank at the door wanting to speak to me! I put on a dressing gown and went down, and there was my friend of the night before.'

Louis had come to say goodbye to Margaret, once again stressing the point that he felt sure he wouldn't survive. Margaret assured him that he would not be killed, and backed it up with some nonsense about being Cornish and having second sight, which didn't impress him greatly as he had never heard of Cornwall. 'He asked if he could kiss me,' says Margaret, 'and I agreed and said I would pray from him. He went off quite quickly, and I never saw or heard of him again.'

One gets the feeling from the story of Louis, that being young and so far away from home and the people that cared for him and loved him, he just wanted somebody – anybody – to say goodbye too. This tragic episode sheds a certain light on the terrifying ordeal that these men faced.

Margaret also went out with one or two other Americans, one of whom was called Earl Petrie, who claimed that he could sing and play the guitar. However, when one evening he was given the chance to prove this, Margaret thought the experience was awful. 'He also wanted an English girl to take home,' she says, 'but I knew it would not be me!'

Eventually Margaret met a Yank called Bob Carroll, whom she did like very much. They got on well together and had lots of fun. One evening, fed up with going to the pictures, they went for a walk and got lost. In the dark they seemed to wander around the Somerset lanes for miles, although Margaret was certain they were heading towards the train station. Bob, who was sick and recuperating at Houndstone Camp, became more and more exhausted, so they had to sit down in a hedge for a while. The poor man from Florida had been over on D-Day and wounded, and had just had six feet of his intestine removed due to its being full of shrapnel.

106   A GI enjoys a walk in the woods with two Hampshire girls, Hazel Green on the left and her friend Lillian. The GI was Edward Rossplock, who came from South Bend, Indiana. These woods were used as a shortcut from the bus stop to Tidworth. (Photo: courtesy of Hazel Green)

'When I went back to Cornwall for Christmas,' Margaret concludes, 'Bob said he would meet me off the train on the day I came back to Yeovil, and carry my case. I looked for him on the station, but he wasn't there. He had gone back to France. I heard from him several times after that, but at the end of the war I changed address, and after a while I heard no more.'

When Theresa Denton first met an American pilot nicknamed Buzz in Romford High Street, she was so taken by him, that she took him home to meet her family, and he was so taken with them, that he stayed for over a year. He proved to be a great help to the family, bringing extra food to their table. The children loved him and he enjoyed all the attention. Theresa remembers him running down the road when a doodlebug fell in the street, lifting an old lady from the ruins of her house, and aiding her until the ambulance arrived. 'Life was never dull when Buzz was around;' she reflects, 'my brother and sisters thought he was wonderful: I did too!'

During the war Theresa worked as a coil winder in a factory which manufactured radar equipment, which at the time was highly secretive. She remembers soldiers coming to the factory and being locked in a huge cage, but admits that at 17 she didn't have a clue what was going on. Buzz, on the other hand, would sometimes fly high-ranking American officers to the Isle of Man, as the island was not subjected to rationing. He was able to return with all manner of delights. He brought Theresa a bracelet with the three-legged emblem of the island and the motto 'Whatever way you throw me, I will stand.'

In time Buzz was posted to France, but still kept in touch with the family by letter, and was even able to visit them for occasional weekends. Theresa met other Americans while dancing and found them 'all very sweet and charming', but admits to being disappointed that when Buzz eventually went back to Milwaukee, he didn't say goodbye.

Sixty years ago Peggy Holbrow was in love with her GI, Private First Class Kenneth Chapman, 'and he loved me', she says. They met at the US Army hospital in Bishops Lydeard where her friend Elsie's cousin Bertie was being treated for gangrene on a wounded leg. Ken, who was also being treated at the hospital, escorted Peggy and Elsie each time they visited her cousin.

107 Hilda Willsone in ATS uniform. She found the Americans 'well behaved' and in her experience they usually just wanted someone to talk to about their folks back home. (Photo: courtesy of Hilda Willsone)

108 Theresa Denton, on the left, was very taken with an American pilot called Buzz, and in this photograph she wears a set of pilot's wings that he had given her, and the bracelet on her left wrist which he had brought back from the Isle of Man. Also in the photograph are Theresa's sister Jessie and brother Philip, who had spent the entire war in a German prisoner-of-war camp. This photo was taken only three days after his return to England and Theresa notes, 'I thought how well he looked after the hell he went through.' (Photo: courtesy of Theresa Denton)

'There was something electric in our meeting,' Peggy explains of their first encounter, 'and our love grew from then on.'

Peggy played the piano and was often asked to liven things up at the local country pub. Tunes such as *She'll be coming round the mountain* and *Yankee Doodle Dandy* helped to raise the spirits of the wounded GIs.

In time, further casualties arrived and beds were needed. Ken was sent to the army base at Blandford in Dorset and the couple met up for a wonderful reunion in nearby Bournemouth.

'We were so happy in each other's company,' says Peggy, 'but it had to end until his next furlough. My Auntie who lived on the Isle of Wight invited me to bring him to Sandown. We stayed with her for seven days – it was such fun – beautiful weather and VJ Day arrived. Despite food and drink shortages – we all went mad – dancing, hugging, kissing; the girls plastered his uniform with lipstick – what did it matter the war was over.'

After their trip to the Isle of Wight, Ken returned to Blandford well aware that the time for his departure was getting ever closer. The depth of his feelings and the strength of his love for Peggy are beautifully expressed in the letters he sent her at that time, such as the following example dated 25 August 1945:

> My Dearest:
> You are so far from me, yet for some unaccountable reason I feel as though you are beside me, not for just a moment, but always. Thanks for those sweet words in your letter received today; don't ever stop telling me of your feelings as I've got to the stage where I feel as though I couldn't do without them. Honestly darling, you've become so much a part of me that I dread even the thought of us ever saying goodbye, but then i've always known that I did find the real thing even though I was lost. I'll always love the memory of those wonderful days that we had together, and they will somehow compensate for the days and nights that will have to be spent without you; you'll always be with me honey, for always and always deep down in my heart, which is now and will always be yours.

I've got sad news honey – I'm very much afraid that I'll be unable to see you in London on the 3rd as I previously mentioned, as things have started to stir. Another outfit consisting of 400 men moved in here the other day, which means extra work on our part as they will be using our facilities and I've been told that my pass would be out of the question. I'm going to keep working on it however, and if I'm not able to process it at that time I'll make it for a later date. I've got to see you soon and tell you over and over again how much I love you, and also to look into your adorable eyes which have haunted me both day and night; particularly at night when I'm lying in bed and thinking of wonderful you.

I suppose that you are now a real hard working gal with nothing on your mind but business – I'll have to disturb those thoughts and give you a ring one morning

109 Peggy Holbrow fell in love with her GI, Kenneth Chapman, after meeting him in the US Army hospital at Bishops Lydeard. (Photo: courtesy of Peggy Holbrow)

soon. To think of you is wonderful; to talk to you would be thrilling; to hold you in my arms and kiss you would be divine; but to hear you say that you love me, is something beyond my wildest comprehension. Darling, I do love you sincerely and long for you with all my heart – you do believe me don't you? Honestly, I've never had this feeling before and know now that it can make one as unhappy as it can happy, and I intend to take my happiness while I can.

Ken Chapman left England in September 1945, having asked Peggy to marry him several times. Although she loved him desperately, she was afraid that she would never see her mother, family and friends again. She had only known Ken in uniform and admits to being apprehensive of starting a new life in Connecticut, so far away from home. As the years roll on, from time to time Peggy still wonders, 'Did I do the right thing in turning him down?'

Honourable intentions

Peggy Braybrooke was born in 1935 in Headington, close to the Churchill Hospital, built by the Americans to care for their injured troops. Her mother had the burden of having female 'war workers' billeted with her. Most of these girls were about 18 years old and came from the area around Stony Stratford (now Milton Keynes). They had been recruited to repair aircraft or to help manufacture munitions in the Morris Motors factory in Cowley.

One of these girls, who came from Old Stratford, was called Betty. The Griffiths family next door had another two girls billeted with them and, further down the road, a girl called Ada lodged with the Giles family.

'Naturally,' explains Peggy, 'the Americans who frequented the public houses at the end of the road and the dance halls in Oxford became friendly with our girls. It was a tortuous journey to get back to Stratford at weekends, so most girls stayed here. Betty, our girl, became very friendly with an American called Max Sellars. He often came to our house where he was welcomed as one of the family. Mind you, at first I had to act as gooseberry until my mother (who considered herself in loco parentis) decided that his intentions were honourable!'

Max was a very friendly man, who brought stockings for Peggy's mother and Betty; and chewing gum for Peggy herself, which she remembers was Juicy Fruit, the likes of which she had never tasted before. 'When it was my 8th or 9th birthday,' Peggy recalls with pride, 'Max had a beautiful cake made for me, covered with chocolate and coloured icing roses. I had never tasted anything so good!'

The relationships between the Americans and these various war workers differed considerably. Ada, who had been courting a chap called Bill, announced that she was getting married. 'I think she was probably pregnant!', suggests Peggy. The couple were married at All Saints Church, and Betty was one of the bridesmaids, wearing a mauve dress. Peggy's mother, and many other people in the road, made things to complement the small reception held at the house of Mrs Giles. 'I believe Ada and Bill were reunited after the war and she went to America and had four sons.'

After leaving for the European battlefields, Max corresponded with Betty for a while, but then the letters stopped coming, and she never knew whether he had been wounded, returned home, or even killed. Of course once the war was over, the girls went back to their own homes, and in due course Betty married a local man and had two daughters.

Dorothy Stanley met Karl Miller, an American airman, in 1942 and the couple went out together until he returned to America in 1945. Karl, who was a master sergeant and responsible for the armaments on Flying Fortresses, was stationed at Deenethorpe in Northamptonshire. Dorothy describes Karl as 'very polite and well mannered'. Her parents regarded him with great affection and he more or less made himself at home in their house during his stay in England.

For a good night out and a chance to meet local girls, the GIs from Deenethorpe would sometimes walk to Weldon and from there catch a bus to Kettering, which was where Dorothy and her parents lived and where the couple first met.

'The arrival of the Americans brought a new and exciting dimension into the lives of young girls,' Dorothy admits. 'I was 20 years old at the time, and now both Karl and I are in our 80s, but we still keep in touch. I have some wonderful memories of that period in my life. His mother used to send me parcels. I remember receiving a bottle of Avon perfume in one, which was lovely. Avon was unheard of in this country then.'

In time Dorothy met and married an Englishman, and Karl married an American girl and went to live in Johnstown, New York. Both have since lost their respective partners and now write and ring each other regularly, recounting memories of what for both of them were among the happiest days of their lives.

American boys and English girls met in many different ways, not just at dances and pubs as commonly perceived. For instance, Joy Wilkinson met four young men – Joe, John, Bob and Jack – through St Francis Church in Salisbury, when it was arranged that members of the congregation would invite Americans to their homes for a Sunday evening meal.

'My Dad was horrified,' notes Joy, 'he believed all the tales about the Yanks! But my friend across the road had a brother in the RAF, and their parents thought it was a great idea, and asked me across to help entertain them. They were four lovely boys, from the Baltimore area, in the same unit, stationed on Salisbury Plain. We had tea and supper with them, listened to classical music, played Monopoly, listened to them talk about their families, and looked at photos of course – Bob was married and had two children, the other three were single. This became a regular Sunday evening date, and we grew very fond of them. They sometimes brought food to eke out the rations, I went out with Joe once or twice – Dad was still horrified, as I had already met the boy I was to marry, though we hadn't told anyone of our plans. My boy was in the RAF, and also stationed on the Plain.'

After the Yanks were shifted west, in preparation for the Normandy invasion, Joy and Joe corresponded, but following D-Day the letters ceased. Much later he wrote again, explaining that they had all taken part in the battle for Omaha Beach. Jack, Bob and John had all been killed on the beachhead, but he had managed to escape himself, though he was missing his mates terribly. For a while they continued to write, but then, as with Betty and Max, the letters stopped coming, and Joy could only assume that he had now been either killed himself, or had simply lost interest.

Olive Martin's sister was 17 and met a very nice young GI at Tidworth barracks, who had just had his 19th birthday. During the early summer of 1945 he was with the family all the time, as they lived near the barracks. He was with a tank division and went on the invasion. She was writing to him every day. Olive clearly remembers one Saturday afternoon when a pile of letters came through the letterbox and, as her father picked them up, without thinking he remarked, 'These are stamped "deceased"'. Her sister cried out, 'Those are my letters to Chick!' Olive will never forget that afternoon and her anguish. A few months after that, one of his friends, now back in the country, came to see her as he thought she didn't know Chick had died. He identified the family from a photograph Chick was carrying in his wallet, and obviously recognised them from his time at Tidworth. Olive's sister had also been in contact with Chick's family in the USA for some time and his sister wrote to say he had been buried in his home town. But his mother never recovered from his death.

110 Dorothy Stanley and Karl Miller, who met in 1942 while he was stationed at Deenethorpe. The couple went out with each other until he returned to the States in 1945. (Photo: courtesy of Mike Stanley)

Bunny Hempsted was in the Land Army for a while and stationed at what was then a very small village – Coggeshall, in Essex. They were 42 accommodated in a country mansion, loaned to the agricultural society for the duration of the war. Although there was a US Army airbase a few miles away, they rarely saw any of the men in the village for there was no entertainment: only about three pubs. Sometimes the girls would go into one of these pubs for a shandy and, on the odd occasion that there were Americans in the bar, they would have drinks sent over to them, out of politeness and respect. Other than that, they made no further advances towards the girls. Then one day, one of the girls had a birthday party in the lounge and invited quite a number of US Army friends. They were found to be very good company and polite, plus very generous when buying drinks. Bunny and one of the other girls made very good friends with two of the boys called Jack and Goldie, 'and', she stresses, 'it was just friendship'.

There were times when some of the Land Army girls would go to work in the fields near the airbase and two or three soldiers would come out to the field, to give them cookies, candy, or cigarettes. They were just being polite, and Bunny states it was evident that they admired the girls for the hard work they were doing for the war effort. Eventually all the girls were invited to the base for a dance and were picked up by lorries. Bunny was greatly impressed by the full-size band. The place was heaving, full of soldiers, and many other girls besides themselves.

She was asked to dance, but refused in the first instance, until being informed that the man she had refused was known to be 'one of the finest jivers in the States'. After a while he asked her again and, being a keen dancer, Bunny this time agreed. 'I was thrown here, there, and up in the air,' she recalls, 'and had great fun.'

Bunny and her friend Eileen would see Jack and Goldie as often as possible, with never a word or hand out of place: they were just very good company. Then, much to their surprise, Matron said they could invite some of the GIs back to the 'hostel' as they called it. Being a mansion house there was a very large reception hall along the whole of the back of the building plus a dance floor and a grand piano. So Bunny got in touch with someone at the base, and invited quite a number of the airmen over. The Americans arrived with a load of drink,

111   Hazel Green, who came to know many Americans stationed near her village of Appleshaw. She sometimes played the piano in the village pub and the GIs would sing along. Their favourite song was 'Don't sit under the apple tree with anyone else but me.' (Photo: courtesy of Hazel Green)

112   A pensive-looking American soldier at Tidworth, perhaps thinking of what lay ahead? He was one of the many GIs that Hazel Green became friendly with. (Photo: courtesy of Hazel Green)

cookies, candy, and even a five-piece band.

'Of course they lashed Matron up with goodies,' states Bunny, 'but she didn't join in with us.' The Land Army girls were supposed to be entertaining the Americans, but the guests did all the entertaining instead, and everyone had a fantastic time.

'I cannot speak too highly of the friendship, respect, and genero-sity of the American Army Air Force,' she concludes. 'They were so out-going and natural, whilst some British people ran them down. As for myself, I came home on weekend leave to find my sister very ill. She was taken to hospital but sadly passed away. So for the sake of my parents, I had to come out of the Land Army. Then, having learned where we lived, Jack and Goldie made a point of coming to see me out of concern. It was just a short visit, but to those who ran the US soldiers down I say, "put that in your pipe and smoke it".'

OVERSEXED AND OVER HERE

Of course, as stated at the start of this chapter, there are two sides to every story and not all English girls were awe-struck by the Americans. Many did and still do feel very differently about them.

Dorothy Smith joined the WRNS in 1943 and reported to their huge receiving depot at Mill Hill in North London. From there the girls were selected for various jobs, depending on their abilities. Dorothy had a university degree, which included advanced German, so she was sent to Wimbledon to do an intensive course in the reception of German R/T on VHF sets. After completion of this she was

113 Local girls with GIs outside the Cadre Club, Tidworth, where Hazel Green (9th from left and wearing white shoes) would go to dances organised by the Red Cross. Hazel explains that the GI on the extreme left of the photo was a chap called Lee Purvis, who played piano in the GI band, and was friendly with Diana Dors. (Photo: courtesy of Hazel Green)

114 'The night of the big Fracas.' This George Rarey cartoon shows GI 'Guys' and local 'Dolls' having a ball at Wormingford. But as it's dated 28 December 1943, I guess they were entitled to a few bevies!! (Illustration: courtesy of Linda Rarey and the EAA Museum)

115   A scene at the American Officers' Bar, The Hells Angels Club, at Molesworth. (Photo: courtesy of 303rd Bomb Group Association/George T. Mackin)

finally posted to various cliff-top outposts along the Welsh and English coasts, from where intercepts were made of all live German in British waters. 'Any operational stuff,' she says, 'was sent to Bletchley Park for decoding.'

During standoff, or while on leave, the girls would head for London. 'We encountered Yankee troops everywhere,' she notes, 'and I'm afraid our impression was not very good – they were brash, cheeky, cocky and sexy, and we avoided them like the plague. They flooded the centre of London, hailing taxis that our own servicemen couldn't afford. We girls would have been ashamed to be seen with any of them. As for our own men, they loathed the sight of them, after all, we had been fighting Hitler for over three years.'

But Dorothy's unfavourable encounters with GIs didn't end there. She would meet them again after volunteering for overseas service. Twelve Special Duty Wrens, of whom Dorothy was one, were sent to Bletchley Park to do a Japanese language course for two months prior to being shipped out on a troopship to Colombo in Ceylon. This was quite an experience: 60 Wrens and 6,000 British troops. However, when they docked at Suez, they observed a flotilla of American landing craft making its way towards them.

'I shall never forget looking down from B Deck,' she recalls, 'as one of the Americans looking up yelled, "Gee – Dames!" The whole flotilla then looked up and simultaneously bawled, "Gee – Dames!"'

Humiliated, and made to feel like some kind of object of desire, all the Wrens quickly retired to their cabins. British troops witnessing this event were understandably furious, and when the Americans were eventually allowed up to their deck, each girl was escorted everywhere by four or five protective Brits.

'During our two years in Colombo,' she concludes, 'a Yankee Naval Task Force came through, spending about a week in port. Wrens refused to go to their dances or to their canteen in town, until our chief officer commanded us to do so. Meanwhile, our camp was daily besieged by hordes of yelling Yanks, trying to get to meet the girls, much to the fury of our Naval guards. Of course there must have been many charming Americans, but this was our experience.'

Mary Singleton and her friends were student nurses at the Bristol Royal Infirmary from 1942-5. She can't remember exactly when the US troops arrived in the city, only that they certainly made a big impression. At that time segregation had to be instigated in Bristol, and the black and white GIs were allocated separate pubs to drink in.

'Unfortunately for us,' she stresses, 'we had to pass several pubs on our way from the nurses' accommodation to the infirmary. It was quite scary, especially for blonde girls, whom they used to chase through the streets. It was said that the local girls preferred the black men as they had better manners. Many fights broke out when white soldiers saw black

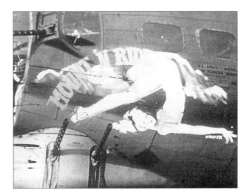

116 Some of the nose art painted on American aircraft made their intentions towards women in some instances seem less than honourable. This B–17G of the 323rd Bomb Squadron, 91st Bomb Group at Bassingbourn, was named 'Mount 'n Ride.' It leaves little to the imagination, and this sort of thing certainly wouldn't have been seen on a British aircraft. (Photo: copyright Paul Chryst)

GIs with white girls, and the MPs would be called. It wasn't long before a crop of mixed-race babies began to appear! Many of them were cared for by the nuns at St Joseph's Home, Cotham.'

Slightly in their defence Mary points out, 'The American servicemen, who were very young, and a long way from home, certainly did "come on strong," but they were used to co-education, and we were not. Except for the elementary schools, where children left at 14, and Quaker schools, nearly all education was single-sex, and girls were closely supervised.'

One thing which history tends to overlook is just how young some of the English girls must have been as they dated American visitors. As Mary Singleton points out, most girls left school and began full-time employment at fourteen. Today, a 14-year-old is still considered to be a child. When the war broke out, Peggy Stephens, who was born and raised in Stourport-on-Severn, a small town in Worcestershire, was only 11, but by 1945 she had risen to the grand old age of seventeen.

Two American military hospitals, the 114th and 297th, were built on a large area of countryside previously occupied by Romany gypsies. The site was undoubtedly selected because it was dissected by the railway line that ran between Stourport and Bewdley. This would be essential for bringing in the weekly hospital trains following the invasion. The line was clearly visible from Peggy's house, and she and her mother would stand and watch as trains moved slowly towards the Burlish Crossing where the ambulances waited to take the wounded up to the hospitals.

'I can see as clearly today as I could then,' she ponders, 'men with their heads bound with bandages, arms in slings etc. and obviously other injuries below the waist which we could not see. Those that could wave did and we responded. It was the first time that most of the residents of our little town had seen first-hand the tragedy of war and seeing those young men minus arms and legs made us realise that they were like this because they had fought for our country.'

On Sundays the Women's Institute became responsible for getting volunteers to go to the hospitals to roll bandages. There was no shortage of volunteers, who were rewarded with chocolate, bananas and nylon stockings. The girls were also invited to Saturday night dances, and were supervised by ladies from the WI. Each girl had to give her name before being counted on to the trucks, which had been sent to ferry them to the hospitals. At the end of the evening they would be counted back on to the trucks again, to make sure they were all there. Needless to say, there was the odd occasion when someone was missing and everyone had to wait while a search took place to find the culprit.

'The average age of those attending the dances was 14 to 15 years,' explains Peggy, 'but as everyone of my generation knows, we were forced to leave school at 14, unless you were at a Grammar school and then the leaving age was sixteen. At 14 years I was working from 8.30a.m. until 5.30p.m. each day plus every other Saturday morning until 12 noon. Yes, we grew up very quickly in those days in more ways than one and our parents did not turn a hair when we visited the camps or dated some of the hundreds of Americans that strolled into town every night. Despite the fact that the blackout procedure meant there were no street lights – in fact there were no lights at all anywhere – it was rare that women were attacked or abused which was due to the very strict discipline administered by the American Military Police.'

The less honourable activities of some GIs left a plague of condoms, seemingly strewn around the streets of England, which again has never been equalled in history. This in itself is a good indication that a certain amount of sexual activity was taking place, whenever and wherever the opportunity arose. Jean Angel, who lived at Great Yeldham in Essex, near the airbase at Ridgewell, says that her mother became very worried about the 'French letters on the paths and roads', in fear of children picking them up and blowing into them, mistaking them for balloons. In the end, with the support of other mothers, she wrote to the local public health department and things improved greatly.

Her fears are given credibility by Ron Green, who as a boy lived near the airbase at Deopham in Norfolk, where the Americans used two local gravel pits as rubbish dumps. Ron explains that 'Us younger children were in agreement that American kids must have had colourless Christmases because all the balloons we kept finding in these pits were colourless off-white ones. There were no red or blue ones, and what was most peculiar was that there were no round ones either, just straight ones about six inches long. We'd fill then full of water and hang them by our desks. The teacher would go potty.' When given an explanation as to the use of these balloons, the children were further confused, as although they lived in the country and knew how rabbits and puppies came into the world, they couldn't understand why anybody or anything should want to prevent babies being born.

At Norton Fitzwarren in Somerset, John Griffin, who was a boarder at Taunton School, remembers many Sunday afternoons when the pupils were allowed out for country walks. Passing the gates to the American camp, the boys noticed how the GIs would hang used French Letters on the chain link fence after their successful sorties. This somewhat distasteful display must have done PR wonders between the Yanks and the local male population.

Looking back, perhaps it isn't that hard to understand why the Americans were so successful with British girls. Bernard Peters, who lived in Truro at the time, makes the point: 'Because of Hollywood films we loved the Yanks before they even got here. When they arrived they were idolized and the girls threw caution to the wind; they went overboard for them and these young Americans were rewarded with what we (the British boys) only dreamed about. Our women folk in the 1940s couldn't get nylons from the shops, not for love nor money, but the Yanks had plenty of them and for "love" the ladies would get them.'

Bryan Keeping, who lived in Poole, where the Americans were based in Branksome Park, recalls that one of his close friends had an attractive older sister who, along with her friends, was dating the visiting soldiers. They had a lot of money and were a breath of fresh air to the English society of the time. Yet Bryan feels that these girls were, without justification, regarded by some as 'easy,' a situation arising because of the outgoing personalities of the visitors and their need for company.

It was difficult, therefore, for any local men who were not away in the forces to date girls while the Americans were around. H. Cox, for instance, worked for a building contractor on the small airfield at Charmy Down just north of Bath. At the time an American Air Force group, the 4th Tactical Air Depot, followed by the 422nd Night Fighter Squadron, 9th USAAF, equipped with the P-61 Black Widows, was stationed there, the latter of which finally vacated the site in October 1944. The GIs would come into Bath when they had time off. 'The girls we used to go out with and were friends with left us and went out with the GIs,' reflects Mr Cox, 'much to our regret, as the Yanks had plenty of money to spend on them. As teenagers we used to go to dances

117   303rd officers entertaining young ladies at the Hells Angels 2nd Birthday bash, 25 September 1944. (Photo: courtesy of Mark Forlow)

at the Pavilion Hall in town, but the Yanks would come in, ask the girls to dance and teach them how to jitterbug etc. So we had to sit back and watch.'

Some of the Americans were already either married or engaged to girls back in the States. These men were, therefore, simply out for what they could get, and certainly did live up to the reputation of being 'Oversexed and over here'. Margaret Ball, for example, who lived in Exeter says: 'When they took a girl to the cinema they would drop a Hershey bar in her lap and she would be delighted. I was 21 that year and I had a very handsome GI boy friend called Ralph. It was six months before he accidentally let slip the words "my wife" and I realised he was married. I stopped seeing him after that, which was made easy by the fact that his unit was sent to Perranporth in Cornwall to train for the D-Day landings.'

118   George Rarey's cartoon of the excitement caused by the arrival of the mail, although by the look on their faces, and the pulsating love-hearts, the letters weren't sent from their moms. (Illustration: courtesy of Linda Rarey and The EAA Museum)

Mrs E. McPace was sent to Rugby, in Warwickshire, to do war work in a munitions factory. On Saturday nights she and her friends would meet at the local pubs, before going on to dances at the church hall, where a lovely little band would play. They all had a great time she recalls until 'they arrived, and all hell broke loose'.

'They spent money like water in the pubs,' she explains, 'and our poor chaps didn't stand a chance. The Yanks uniform was wonderful, and they all seemed to come from Hollywood, so the girls fell at their feet. Girls were losing their virginity to them left, right and centre. These girls proudly wore the gold "tie pin" given to them by a Yank the next day. The girls would even have the date of their de-flowering put on the pin.'

Even though all of this was going on around her, Mrs McPace admits to having many good memories of the Americans because she enjoyed their company without getting involved. She was engaged to a 'beautiful' English boy, whom she would later marry.

CHAPTER 8

GI BRIDES AND BABIES

For many American servicemen, due to their tender years, romances with British girls would have been their first experience of serious relationships, even though they were often conducted at whirlwind speed. These relationships were often physically and emotionally more passionate than they might normally have been, because of the circumstances under which they were formed. Marriages were also entered into at breathtaking speed, and the reason why these Anglo-American unions are important, is because of the children that resulted from them. These children, and today's grandchildren and great-grandchildren, are a tangible link in the history that unites two nations.

For many girls in Britain, marriage to a GI must have seemed like a fairytale come true. But in reality, were there happy endings to such fairytales? As with most of the subjects so far addressed, the answer to this question is both 'Yes' and 'No.' On reaching America many girls discovered that their seemingly wealthy husband actually lived in virtual poverty. And far from living in Hollywood or Manhattan, many lived in remote, isolated backwaters of the mid-west. On the other hand, many marriages were a tremendous success and have lasted from that day to this in perfect happiness.

Going state side

One of the very first war brides must surely have been Hilda Paull, who married her husband Stephen in January 1942. A group of Americans interested in electronics had been sent to Richmond in Surrey, where at the time people were working on the development of Radar, or RDF as it was known in Britain. The group came over in September 1941 to learn about the British system, with a view to returning to America to teach it. 'It was fairly hush-hush,' explains Hilda, 'and the Americans didn't wear uniforms.'

Stephen Paull, who came from upper Michigan, was one of these American electronic experts, and while he was here the Japanese attacked Pearl Harbor. By this time Stephen was stationed with an English company of the Signal Corps in Cornwall, but he had already met Hilda while in Richmond where her parents lived.

After a short romance, the couple married on 19 January 1942, and although this might seem very sudden, the circumstances have to be taken into consideration, as Hilda explains: 'I was probably one of the

119   Betty Traves was the bridesmaid at the wedding of her friend Marjorie to her special Yank Bill in 1945. Marjorie was in the ATS, and the couple went to the States after the war, after which Betty lost contact with them. (Photo: courtesy of Betty Traves)

first war brides. We were married at that time because we thought I would be going back with him when he returned to the US.'

However, she soon resigned herself to the fact that the 'best made plans often go awry'. With America coming into the war, instead of going home to Michigan, Stephen was posted to North Africa, and afterwards to Italy. She didn't see him again for the next two years.

Marrying a GI was not an easy route to America, as there was a strict immigration policy, and many wives couldn't get their ticket until several years after the end of hostilities. With limited transport available across the Atlantic, there was a quota system in place. Hilda had the advantage of working in London, so in January 1944 she went to the American Embassy to see if she could get on the quota. She must have applied at the right time, as she was told that, following the necessary health checks, she could go immediately.

Although her husband was still in Europe, she had nothing to lose and says, 'I thought why not, my husband was a captain and he paid my fare. I was told to report to Euston Station at 7a.m. I can't remember the date, as all my papers were censored.'

Living in Richmond, it would have been difficult to get to Euston by 7a.m., especially at a time when the Germans were still bombing the city. So, having said goodbye to her family, Hilda spent the night at the office where she worked in Aldwych. On arriving at the station, she met one other war bride and about four or five American civilians making their way home. There were also some 250 wounded American soldiers aboard.

120 Sergeant Leonard Dougal, who was a tail gunner based in Norfolk, and Gertrude 'Cissy' Wilkins. They met in Norwich on Easter Sunday in 1943, and were married in March 1944. After the war they lived happily together in the United States. (Photo: courtesy of Gwen Kemp)

'I had never been anywhere,' she explains, 'and here I was sitting on Euston Station not knowing where I was going. We boarded the SS *Brazil* at Liverpool, formerly of the United Fruit Lines. There were 24 ships in the convoy. We used to help with some of the wounded, sit and watch for periscopes and the destroyers. We ate breakfast at 7a.m., lunch at 11a.m., and dinner at 4p.m. The food was quite a revelation – white bread and huge pieces of butter. We were due to land in New York but two days out we were told we would be landing in Boston instead. The doctor booked the other bride and myself into a hotel.'

Bearing in mind that in London there was a total blackout, one of Hilda's first recollections of Boston was running along the street laughing as the lights came on. She initially made her way to New York, where she stayed for a while as she had connections there from when she had worked at the Red Cross American Officers Club in London. After this she journeyed to Detroit to meet her brother-in-law and his wife. Finally, after changing trains at Chicago, she made her way to upper Michigan, to meet her in-laws. 'For somebody who had never been anywhere,' she reiterates, 'I certainly went somewhere.'

There was very little news of the war filtering through to people in America, and having no word of her husband and to avoid the cold winter of upper Michigan, she went down to Milwaukee in September 1944. She was there when Stephen returned at the end of October, and the couple were finally reunited at Falls Church, Virginia, just outside Washington DC.

After leaving the Army, Stephen Paull worked at the Naval Research Laboratories in Maryland. The couple had one daughter together before Hilda returned to England in 1961 following a divorce.

Similar to Hilda Paull, the end result of most Anglo-American marriages saw the GI bride eventually joining her new husband in the United States of America. Many examples could be quoted, such as the marriage of Sergeant Leonard Dougal, who was a tail gunner in a Liberator Squadron, the 328th based at Hardwick in Norfolk, and

121 Tangible links: Charles 'Chuck' Osborn (left), who was stationed in Devon during the Second World War, and married local girl Hilda Manley, with his daughter Deb and her husband, and grandson Luke. (Photo: courtesy of Ken Manley)

Gertrude 'Cissy' Wilkins. They met in Norwich on Easter Sunday in 1943, and were engaged a month later. In November Sergeant Dougal requested official permission to marry and they finally sealed the knot in March 1944.

Sergeant Dougal had a distinguished career with the Air Corps, completing 25 bombing missions. He took part in the longest mission of the war, a 17-hour run from Bengasi to Wiener-Neustadt. He was awarded the Air Medal with four Oak Leaf Clusters, the presidential citation, and the Distinguished Flying Cross with Oak Leaf Cluster.

After the end of hostilities, Dougal went back to his home in Detroit, but Cissy was unable to join him immediately because of the ban on civilian travel. Going to the United States must have been a daunting prospect anyway for someone who had lived in Norwich all her life and had never even been as far as London before. But with the eventual lifting of the civilian travel ban and the help of the American Consul, the two were finally reunited.

Cissy's niece, Mrs Gwen Kemp, who still lives in Norwich, explains that Leonard Dougal became a police officer in Detroit after the war, and when he retired the couple moved to Sarasota, where they spent many happy years together. Cissy died in October 2003.

Ken Manley's sister Hilda also married her American sweetheart in 1945. She was born in Barnstaple in north Devon, where in 1943 she met a handsome young army corporal, Charles Osborn, at a local dance hall. She was 16 and he was 19 years old. She loved to jitterbug and Charles was an expert. Charles was staying at the hutted camp at Braunton on the Devon coast, part of the US Army Assault Training

Centre. Hilda gave Charles the nickname 'Short' undoubtedly due to his stature, but Ken prefers to call him 'Chuck'. The courtship began, and while watching a movie together, *Hello, Fresco, Hello Fresco*, in which Alice Faye sang the song *You'll never know*, they lovingly looked into each other's eyes and knew it was love. They married on 9 June 1945.

As a GI war bride, Hilda journeyed to America in 1947, accompanied by their first son, Alan Lee, who was ten months old. Charles had built their home in Mission Valley, San Diego, where their second son Danny Lee was born. Although Hilda discovered American life to be very different, she soon found her feet, especially after they moved into a brand new home on Aragon Drive, San Diego, where eight years later their daughter Debra Lynn was born.

Sadly, Hilda passed away in August 1999 and a little celebration

122   Don Hetrick, a GI in the 101st airborne, who married Joan Sherman at St Michael's church, Little Bedwyn on 12 March 1945. Joan's friend Myrtle had a small-holding where she kept chickens and turkeys, where this photo was taken. Joan and Myrtle met Don and his friend Walter one evening when they went down to lock up the birds for the night. (Photo: courtesy of Muriel Mundy)

of her life, printed at the time of her Service of Remembrance at the United Methodist Church, Santee, California, includes the following testimony to a strong and successful union: 'A treasured moment was her 50th Anniversary at Charlie Brown's. Hilda and Charles were married for 54 years. He is her prince, her knight in shining armour, who swept her away into his heart forever. Their love and devotion for each other is truly a blessing and will last an eternity.'

Joan Mundy was working on a local farm having joined the Women's Land Army, when the 101st Airborne Division arrived at Froxfield on the border between Wiltshire and Berkshire. Her sister Muriel explains that their parents had a house in the village of Little Bedwyn, and had three daughters. The eldest had joined the WAAFs, while Joan, the middle one of the three, had fallen in love with a GI called Don Hetrick. Before his departure for Normandy, Don asked Joan to marry him. It was all very sudden, so her parents weren't very keen on the idea, having heard many tales of the Americans taking advantage of local women; some they believed to be already married back in the States. Don had to get permission from his CO and a special licence to marry Joan, so before he left she gave her consent, and on his return to England they were married in the church at Little Bedwyn on 12 March 1945. The couple proved her parents wrong as they went to live in America and celebrated 60 years together, before they both passed away.

123 Don and Joan's wedding, at Little Bedwyn church on 12 March 1945. Don and Joan are on the left of the photograph. (Photo: courtesy of Muriel Mundy)

Beryl Reeser met her American husband in Bournemouth, where she lived, while walking along the promenade. They talked of how scarce fruit was and he promised to bring her some oranges. The very next night he was true to his word, bringing her both oranges and sweets. They dated for about six weeks before he was sent back to the United States. They corresponded, until sometime in 1946 when he wrote asking her to marry him. She went to the United States in 1947 where she still lives today in Hummelstown, Pennsylvania. The couple had two sons, four grandchildren and four great-grandchildren. Her husband passed away in 1998, after 51 years of marriage, and Beryl says, 'If I could live my life over again, I would not change a thing.'

The father of Jane Smith, Captain John B. Thomas, was stationed in Parkend in the Forest of Dean during the war. He was in the 263rd Ordnance Ammunition Battalion Headquarters. They received all types of ammunition ranging from small arms to bombs, which they dispatched to anywhere they were needed.

124 John B. Thomas (left), the father of Jane Smith, photographed in September 1944. (Photo: courtesy of Jane Smith)

125   *The New Inn* at Parkend, as it was during the war. Today it has been renamed *The Woodman.* (Photo: courtesy of Jane Smith)

Jane's grandparents, the Bakers, managed a public house just across the green from John's headquarters: the *New Inn*, now called *The Woodman*. On one occasion, when he came into the bar, their daughter, Jane's mother Elizabeth, was having a drink with friends. She had already done service in the Women's Land Army, as a 'saw doctor' working at a sawmill near Ely. John explains, 'When I saw her I made up my mind that I wanted to meet her'.

It so happened that a member of his battalion had married an English girl, who a little while later had come from Cheltenham to stay at the *New Inn* for a week, to be near her husband. One evening she visited the soldiers at their accommodation, the Old Forestry School in Parkend. She told John about a girl she had become friendly with at the inn, and thought they should meet. When she described the girl, he knew straight away it was the same girl he had already seen and needed no persuading.

At a dinner given by his battalion for friends and associates living in the area, which the couple had attended separately, John appeared and removed Elizabeth's plate, saying, 'If you want to eat this you'll have to come sit with me'. She accepted the invitation and after that they were always together. Three weeks later he left for Normandy. He wasn't even able to say goodbye to Elizabeth, and she was heartbroken on learning of his departure.

It was several weeks before Elizabeth heard from John again, because as soon as he landed on the beaches, he had to have an emergency appendectomy. Finally he was able to write and eventually proposed. After all the checks to make sure he didn't have a wife and six kids back in the States, they were allowed to marry. They found that one of John's brothers was in hospital in Cheltenham having been wounded, but he was well enough to attend the wedding as best man. The couple were eventually married at St Paul's Church, Parkend, on 5 June 1945.

As with most other examples, John returned to America, and it wasn't until 1946 that Elizabeth was able to join him. He met her in New York, and the couple lived happily in Tennessee until she died in 1977. Jane, who was born nine months after Elizabeth sailed to America, often

126 John B. Thomas, father of Jane Smith, photographed in September 1944. (Photo: courtesy of Jane Smith)

visited her family in England and on one trip in 1973 she met Gerry. After a whirlwind romance lasting three weeks, that any wartime GI and his bride would be proud of, Jane went home engaged, only to return to England again ten weeks later for her wedding: she's been here ever since.

Deanna Allan, who was born in 1941 in Corby, Northamptonshire, relates the story of her aunt Mary Myles and Sergeant Paul Hafke. There were many airbases around the district: Deenethorpe, Spanhoe and Grafton Underwood amongst them. The service personnel would often cycle into Corby from these bases, or come by Jeep to attend the dances at *The Raven Hotel* or The Welfare Club, as it was the nearest town. Mary was a very pretty lady who for three years running had been the beauty Queen of Corby, and Sgt Hafke, from Waterloo in Iowa, was serving with 316-troupe carrier group attached to the 8th Air Force at Spanhoe. Paul had been a teacher of industrial education before the war, and gained his master's degree on his return to the States. During the war Mary became a nurse in the civil nursing reserve and worked at St Mary Abbot's Hospital in Kensington. She would return home to Corby at the weekends, and first met Paul at a dance held in the Welfare Club: they danced to the music of the Johnny Ballantyne band.

The couple were married on 14 April 1945 at St John the Baptist Church, Corby, with the Reverend Brooke-Westcott officiating at the ceremony. Mary's wedding dress was sent from the groom's family in the States and came from Marshall Fields Department Store in Chicago, costing 100 dollars, a considerable sum at the time.

A week before the wedding, Paul's squadron was transferred from Spanhoe airfield to France but his colonel gave permission

127 Daphne Elizabeth Baker, mother of Jane Smith. (Photo: courtesy of Jane Smith)

128 John and Daphne ten days after their wedding on 15 June 1945. (Photo: courtesy of Jane Smith)

for the wedding to take place as arranged and he managed to hitch a plane back to England in time for his wedding.

One year later, Mary sailed to her new life accompanied by her infant son, Paul Junior, on board the *Queen Mary* with many other war brides, all looking forward to being re-united with their husbands. Arriving to berth in New York amidst much publicity, dozens of smaller boats honked a greeting and a quayside band played *Sentimental Journey*. Flowers were offered to the women in a friendly gesture.

Mary kept in touch with some of the women she sailed with, who formed their own association, The War Brides Association of Iowa, and together they returned for many trips to the UK. In April 2005, Mr and Mrs Paul Hafke celebrated their Diamond Wedding, 60 years of marriage, still living happily together in Waterloo, Iowa.

BACK TO BLIGHTY

Of course not all marriages ended with the bride going to America. In some instances, the groom remained behind, or returned to England when the opportunity arose. Such was the case of Alexander Francis Langraf, the father of Penny Fleming.

Alex Langraf was born in Chicago, Illinois, in 1919. He had just started at university, studying law, when he was called up and joined the Army Air Corps. Because of a physical problem, now diagnosed as a nervous condition due to spinal stenosis, he had a non-combatant role, being drafted to Alconbury in Cambridgeshire to do clerical work as a corporal with the Pathfinders.

On a few days' leave, he went down to Torquay in Devon and met Doris Sylvia Schutte at a tea dance. 'She was not impressed with American GIs,' states her daughter Penny, 'especially those who chewed gum, so she refused to dance with him! However, he persevered and eventually took her and her mother, who accompanied her everywhere, home by taxi.'

After that he was hooked, and spent all his available spare time down on the English Riviera, courting his true love. He would come by train or cadge lifts anyway he could. Penny's grandparents had a guesthouse, and Alex would be allowed to stay there when he arrived in town.

'Eventually,' Penny explains, 'he asked her to marry him. She accepted, but she had to go up to Alconbury to meet his commanding officer, to get his agreement to the marriage. I understand that a little while later she received a telephone call from Alex saying that he had been in an all-night poker game and had won five big diamonds. He had these made into an engagement ring for her.

They married at St Mary Magdalene Church, Upton, Torquay on 17 September 1944. Unfortunately she was not able to wear a white wedding dress, as clothing was rationed and she could not get hold of the relevant material.

Alex was demobbed in 1945 and had to return to the USA for this procedure to take effect. The rest of the story is far from being smooth as, whilst he was away, Doris discovered that she was pregnant with Penny. She sent him a letter, but Penny believes his mother destroyed it, as she was always opposed to the wedding and didn't want her son to return to England, or his wife to join him in America.

'My mother became very worried that she had not heard from him,' continues Penny, 'and was advised by her doctor, a friend, that she should send him a telegram, as this would go directly to my father. She did this and received a telegram straight back, saying that he was "overjoyed at the wonderful news, just turned 17 handsprings etc., etc." I still have the telegram.'

129 Alexander Langraf of Chicago, Illinois, married Doris Schutte of Torquay, Devon, at St Mary Magdalene Church, Upton, Torquay, on 17 September 1944. This photo was taken on their wedding day in the grounds of Trematon, a guesthouse run by the bride's parents. Their reception was at the *Clarence Hotel*, Torquay. (Photo: courtesy of Penny Fleming)

Alex returned to England and, except for one occasion in 1956, when his mother was killed in a car accident, he never went back to the USA again. He asked Doris if she would like to live in the US, but being close to her parents she didn't want to go and Alex respected her wishes.

Alex and his father-in-law set up a toy wholesale business, which they ran from the guesthouse in Torquay, until the death of his mother. The business was sold and with the proceeds of her estate, he bought a large detached Victorian property called Bronshill Court in 1959, which at one time had been owned by John Galsworthy's widow. He converted part of the house into a large three-bedroom flat. In time, two more daughters arrived, Victoria Leslie and Judith Hope.

'After buying and converting Bronshill Court,' says Penny, 'my father also bought an estate agency business and I worked for him for about 12 years, until I had my own first child. In 1972 he built a four-bedroom detached house in the grounds of Bronshill Court to accommodate the whole family, but three days after we moved in, I got married and left. My sister Vicki left about a year later to work in Bermuda and eventually my youngest sister, Judy left to work in Taunton! Some time later he sold off Bronshill Court.'

At one time Alex Langraf was Chairman of the local Chamber of Trade and also Chairman of the local Estate Agency Association. He had a very successful business career in England.

'I had thoughts to go back to work with him at a later date,' concludes Penny, 'but my father became ill with angina, and his spinal stenosis and ensuing arthritis affected his legs, so he sold the business some time in the 1980s and retired. He had a lot of ill health and many operations including open-heart surgery, hernia, back and four hip operations. We used to joke that he was the bionic man! He died on 29 April 1995. My husband and I, and our two children, moved in with mother to look after her, but unfortunately she is now in a residential home in very poor failing health.'

The father of Tim Bliss, Theodore Bliss, although a US citizen, was actually born in Nanking, China in 1918, where his own father was working as a medical missionary. Theodore, who was always known as 'Ted', lived in Nanking until he was seven, when his parents decided to return to New York because of the political situation in China at the time. He later lived in Tokyo for ten years, where his father worked at the general hospital, after which they returned to New York again and the young Theodore attended Cornell University.

Following the attack on Pearl Harbor, he joined the US Army Signal Corps and later served in Iceland, monitoring German U-boat signals, but by early 1944 he was dispatched to Lymington in England where he was stationed at Elmers Court.

Tim's mother, Beryl June Tatton, who was born in 1920 and always known as 'June', lived with her parents and sister Vivienne, at Golden Bush, Boldre near Lymington, and according to family legend Tim says: 'The two sisters were walking home from Brockenhurst station pushing their bicycles, due to June's bicycle having a puncture. Suddenly they heard a voice from behind and two GI's hailed them and walked with them to their home. The next day my father visited Golden Bush and repaired the puncture. Apparently a romance blossomed that led to my parents' wedding in May 1944. After a brief honeymoon my father rejoined his unit and was part of the D-Day landings.'

Tim's father told him that, after VE Day and due to his marriage, he was considered a 'top priority' to be returned to the US. So he was shipped by a devious route, due to the possible danger of rogue U-boats still patrolling the Atlantic, back to the US arriving well after all the 'low priority' troops had returned by more conventional routes.

June was one of the many GI brides who travelled to New York from Southampton, aboard the *Queen Mary*. For a while the couple lived with Theodore's parents in Gramercy Park, New York, and, later, after Vivienne was born, they moved out to Long Island.

After Tim's grandmother Helen suddenly and quite unexpectedly passed away, and his grandfather retired, in 1950, they all came to live in England at Golden Bush where Tim was born in 1952. But with a further increase in the size of the family when Simon Bliss was born in 1956, they all moved to a bigger property at Royden, Brockenhurst.

Tim's father, who while in England worked as an instrument fitter at the Esso Oil Refinery at Fawley neat Calshot, and who was involved in the early computerisation of the monitoring equipment there in the 1960s and early 1970s, died in 1975. His mother died in June 2005 and, after studying at Southampton Polytechnic and starting a career in computer programming, Tim and his own wife Ann went to live in California in 1982. They are still there, living in Freemont, and now have three children of their own: Jennifer, Thomas, and Victoria. But Theodore and his GI bride June are both buried at Boldre Church, near Lymington.

130 Sergeant Jim Sharkey, who met his future wife Annie while she was working in Tidworth on an American switchboard. (Photo: courtesy of Annie Sharkey)

During the war, the family of Annie Sharkey came from Dornoch, Sutherland, to live in Tidworth, as her father was in the reserve. Annie and her best friend Joan went to work at the Ordnance Depot switchboard and were both very young. From July 1943 to August 1945 they worked on an American switchboard which had been brought over from the States. During this time Annie met 'a nice American chap' called Jim Sharkey from New York, who was with the Engineers. After the war he came back from America to serve in France and the couple were married in 1960 in Tidworth, but then lived together in France before coming back to England and living near Salisbury, after Jim had completed 20 years' service. The couple spent 30 happy years together before Jim passed away in 1990. As a coincidence, Annie's sister Chrissie also met her American husband at a dance at Tidworth, Captain Jim Marshall, but they went to live in Roanoke, Virginia.

George John Petroff was an honorary Englishman, born in Manchester, New Hampshire in March 1919. At the entry of the US into the war he was one of the first to volunteer to serve in the US Army Air Force and he was on the second shipment of US personnel to arrive in the UK on the *Queen Mary*. He first served in a bomber squadron and later transferred to 8th Air Force Fighter Command. George was introduced to his future English wife Sheila in 1944 and they were married at Emmanuel Parish Church, Northwood on 4 August 1945.

After an honourable discharge with four medals, he and Sheila returned to the USA, enabling George to continue with his education and obtain a Science degree at New Hampshire University. He returned to the UK in 1951 on a Fulbright scholarship. In 1952 the US Embassy in London gave him a position with Material Command, and he continued to work for the US government in the London area as a liaison officer with the US Air Force.

George lived with his family in Northwood, Middlesex, where his son attended Merchant Taylors' School and his daughter attended Watford Grammar School for Girls. On retirement George and Sheila moved to Highcliffe in Dorset in 1982, a part of the country he was particularly fond of. Sheila explains that her husband died in 1995, three months after their

131 The wedding of Jim and Annie Sharkey at Tidworth in 1960. (Photo: courtesy of Annie Sharkey)

132 The wedding at St John's church, Bath, between Johnnie Kiernan of Montgomery, Alabama, and Christine Haddaway of Hastings, Sussex. Also in the photo is Mrs Garraway, maid of honour at left of photo with large bouquet. It was while staying at her house in Bath that Johnnie first met Christine, who had been evacuated to the Somerset city and was living next door. Also in the photo are the bride's mother, and father (in Merchant Navy uniform). (Photo: Mr T.E. Garraway)

50th wedding anniversary. George loved England and was particularly fond of such customs as afternoon tea and traditional Sunday lunch. He also loved a good old-fashioned English detective story. George also liked the English seaside, to which he took his young family on many happy holidays. This is how he came to love Highcliffe-on-Sea. On retiring he became an active member of the residents' association and joined the neighbourhood watch as a deputy. He was also involved with the Community Centre; the Highcliffe Theatre Group; and the local Conservative Club. In fact, he was probably more of an Englishman than many native-born Brits.

GI BABIES

Penny Fleming and Jane Smith are both GI babies, inasmuch as they were the product of marriages between English girls and American GIs. However, one of the most controversial aspects of 'the friendly invasion', were the numerous illegitimate children that were left behind. This is an extremely delicate issue even now, and a lady wishing to remain anonymous describes the destruction and heartbreak that was left behind for these poor infants. 'I am the product of a liaison between a young American GI and my birth mother, and even now it still hurts a great deal and still feels very unfair. I fully appreciate the difficult times but it does not help the many offspring like myself to come to terms with it. I am aware of my father's name and where he came from. At various times I have tried to track him down to no avail. I have always held back from doing any real research for fear of upsetting his family and causing hurt to others; however, it does not stop my hurt and wondering! Even after all this time it does not get any easier.'

There must be hundreds if not thousands of children that were left in this terrible situation, but at least one such GI baby, Gwendoline Gallech, admits to having 'a very happy ending' to her story, which really begins when her mother Elizabeth was evacuated from the London Blitz to the town of Kettering in Northamptonshire. Elizabeth had four other children from a failing marriage, who were also evacuated to the safety of the countryside, but separately from her.

During this period of relocation, Elizabeth met and began a relationship with a GI called Homer Chambers, who was stationed at Grafton Underwood, where several elements of the 8th Air Force were based. Homer was a sergeant and crew chief, working on B-17 bombers.

As a result of their two-year romance, Gwendoline Rose was born on 7 August 1945, eight months before her father was posted to Germany. To bring him luck, Homer took one of the baby's booties with him.

Undoubtedly, Homer would have married Elizabeth at this time, but she was still married to her first husband Charles, who had been in Africa with the British Army. On returning to England, Charles went to Kettering to see Elizabeth, and found her pushing a pram along the road with Gwen in it, and Homer at her side. Charles offered to take her back and bring Gwen up as his own, but Elizabeth said 'No', as there had been too many problems between them over the years, so

133   Homer Chambers, who was stationed at Grafton Underwood. (Photo: courtesy of Gwen Gallech)

the couple were finally divorced in 1946.

By that time Homer had returned to his home in Texas, with the intention of saving up enough money to bring the family to America. But times were still hard in Britain, and Elizabeth was struggling to cope. She wrote to Homer, asking him to send money to help support her and her family, which now included their baby daughter. Homer simply couldn't afford it, repeating the promise that he would fetch her when the time was right.

When Gwendoline was two-and-a-half years old, and because she was still struggling to make ends meet under very difficult circumstances, Elizabeth married an English suitor Thomas Henley: perhaps by now she had given up all hope of being reunited with the man she loved. However, by a cruel twist of fate, Homer returned shortly afterwards to fetch his first-born child and English sweetheart, only to be told of Elizabeth's marriage, and that he was never to have contact with his daughter again.

Henley had known about Homer but had convinced Elizabeth into thinking that she had been abandoned, and that Gwendoline was merely the result of a frivolous wartime romance. He insisted that, if Homer had really cared for her, he would have sent her at least some of the money she asked for. Henley thereafter adopted Gwen and the couple decided that the girl would never be told the truth, so she grew up in the belief that Thomas was in fact her real father.

'I loved Thomas Henley as my father,' Gwen explains, 'but lacked respect for him. He was an alcoholic, so you can imagine the problems created by that situation.'

When Gwendoline was ten years old, her parents' plan came across a stumbling block. While being enrolled at her local school, the headmistress insisted that the girl should use the legal name on her birth certificate, which was Chambers. Elizabeth and Thomas were faced with the unavoidable prospect of having to tell Gwen about Homer. They even made arrangements for the girl to go and stay with her older sister, in the event that she took the news badly. But as it happened, she was elated!

'I loved it.' Gwen recalls, 'It was ever so special being adopted, because then, my real father became a figment of my imagination. Any time Mum and Dad yelled at me or I got angry with them, he was going to come and rescue me, wherever he may be. With each family argument, and there were quite a few, Homer became more and more my knight in shining armour. I feel the reason Henley cut off contact from my Dad, was not so much in my interest, as to keep him away from Mum. I think she was always in love with Homer.'

In 1970, having grown up dreaming of her Texas family, Gwen married an American soldier herself who was stationed at Alconbury as a fireman, and by coincidence the couple were relocated to Texas. Obviously, the situation brought her to wonder more and more about her real father. She had snippets of information provided by her mother, and her Aunt Rose. His name was Homer Woodrow Chambers, he was still

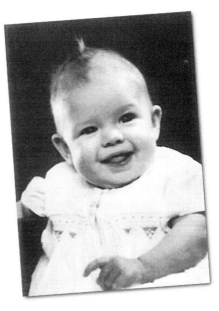

134   Gwen as a baby. (Photo: courtesy of Gwen Gallech)

serving in the American Air Force, and lived somewhere near Dallas. While working in the officers club she would sometimes look at the nametags set out on the table, or in the phone book, hoping to come across his name. The couple moved to Ohio for a spell, but then, after returning to Texas, she decided to begin ringing some of the numbers she had listed.

Calling one of the numbers listed to a Homer W. Chambers, a woman informed her that it was a different man. Gwen told the woman that during the war her family had been friends with Mr Chambers, and she was looking for him because she was researching a book. The woman promised to make some enquiries and ring back, but she didn't. However this experience gave Gwen cold feet, and she did not resume her search having decided in her own mind that she didn't want to interrupt or complicate his life. 'He had quite obviously made another life,' said Gwen, 'and perhaps no one knew about me.'

Time ticked by and in due course Gwen and her husband divorced. She then married her second husband Glen, and settled in Salem.

Suddenly, there was a dramatic twist to the story. Gwen's older sister Iris had been contacted in England by a lady claiming to be the daughter of Homer Chambers, who was looking for her English sister. Soon after, Gwen herself was contacted by a lady called Janet Prato in New York, who acts as an 'icebreaker', bringing people like Gwendoline together again with their families. Before long, Gwen was not only speaking to her sister Aimee, but several other members of her totally new family as well. Sadly though, Gwen was never to meet her father, as Homer had died of cancer in 1978, at the age of 54.

Gwen learned that following his failed attempt to bring her and her mother back to America, Homer had married his wife Dorothy seven years later. Dorothy already had three sons from a previous marriage, and the couple had three daughters together. The more she learned about Homer, it became evident that he had been a wonderful man, that she could be truly proud of. After retiring from the military, he had become a pastor and was a much-loved member of the community.

Aimee had tracked her sister down after finding details in her father's papers. She also learned that he kept photos of her as a baby, in the family album, and celebrated her birthday, every 7 August. Her new family welcomed her with loving and open arms, as though she had been with them all along. Her American sisters had also fantasised about their father rescuing their 'English princess'. He would sit and trace her picture in the photo album with his finger, and it was very clear that he had loved her very much, and must have been heartbroken at their separation.

'Would you believe the Chambers family still had that bootie?', notes Gwen. 'They never knew where it came from. They never knew until I told them.'

Several organisations exist to help people find their GI fathers, one of which is aptly named TRACE (Trans Atlantic Children's Enterprise). All members of this group are either children or grandchildren searching for their American GI fathers or grandfathers, and some, such as Pauline Natividad, have successfully concluded their search.

Pauline was born in Southampton: her father had been a US Army medic based at Winchester, who had met her mother at a local dance. They dated for some time but then her father was sent to France, and afterwards returned home to the USA. When Pauline was only eight, her mother died suddenly and it was decided that she should be raised by her maternal grandparents. Pauline still knew nothing about her father, but remembers asking about him at a very early age. 'Happily,' she relates, 'many years later my lifetime dream came true. I had really thought it to be an impossible quest. But after a long – pre internet – search, I successfully tracked my father down back in 1988 when I was 44 years old. I first spoke to him on a Thursday in November, not realising that it was actually Thanksgiving Day. The next day, when my news came out at work, my co-workers collected for an air ticket for me to visit my father and new family in El Paso, Texas for Christmas.'

Today, Pauline is an officer of TRACE, and uses her experience to help others who find themselves in similar situations.

Earlier, we learned from Mary Singleton that in Bristol the presence of black GIs led to a 'crop of mixed-race babies', some of whom were cared for by nuns at St Joseph's Home in Cotham. When a white English girl was made pregnant by her black American boyfriend, the result could only have been a tragedy. Relationships between black men and white women were illegal in the United States. Therefore, no matter how much the couple loved each other, they could never get married and return to the States as a happy couple.

St Joseph's was only one of several homes to look after mixed-race babies after the war, another being Holnicote House, near Bridgwater in Somerset, where Deborah Prior spent her early years. In 2005 Deborah celebrated her 60th birthday at her home in Brisbane, Australia, and received through the post a wonderful surprise: a birthday card signed by some of the most important women in her life. These were women who had cared for her decades before, who had wiped her tears and changed her nappies when she had nobody else. They had been the teenage nurses at Holnicote House, who had taken care of so many unwanted children at the end of the war, yet Deborah feels 'they are still watching over me'.

Ruth Wood, reporter with the *Western Daily Press*, produced a wonderful article about Deborah on the occasion of her 60th birthday, in which she wrote, 'Deborah was one of a wartime generation dubbed the "brown babies", the daughter of a black American soldier stationed in Somerset and a Bridgwater woman'.

Such was the stigma of having a mixed-race baby in 1940s Britain that Deborah was wrenched away from her mother's arms shortly after her birth. She spent the first five years of her life at Holnicote House, being looked after by trainee nurses. There were 40 children at the home at the time, of whom 20 were of mixed race. Of this period in her life Deborah said, 'My memories of Holnicote are nothing but happy – playing in the garden, the little pond, the dressing-up games and doll house. We went on a walk every day and we had to wear boots.'

Deborah was adopted at the age of five, and even though critics at the time claimed that the 'brown babies would never amount to anything', she at least proved them wrong. No doubt influenced by the kindness of the Somerset nurses who, as Ruth Wood writes, 'kissed and cuddled her through infancy', people like Mary Hebditch and others, Deborah became a nursing lecturer and completed a PhD in medical anthropology. She married, moved to Australia, had three children, and is now director of learning and development at the Centre for Palliative Care, Research and Education in Brisbane. If that's not making a success of your life from such tragic beginnings, then surely nothing is!

CHAPTER 9

'Got any gum chum?'

In researching this book, the phrase most commonly remembered by quite literally hundreds of people is, 'Got any gum chum?' This phrase was used by children from Cornwall to Kent, or wherever else GIs might have been based, as a customary request for any freebies that the generous Yanks might pass their way. So far we have studied the many different relationships that were forged between the two allies, such as those with the people the Americans met socially, were accommodated with, worked with, romanced, or even married. But they also had a very special bond with English children, who benefited regularly from their generous nature.

As the British and their new American neighbours became more accustomed to each other's presence, the two sides came into ever-closer contact. In time, not only were the Americans welcomed into British homes, but the locals, normally children, would visit the Yanks in theirs. In theory these American camps should have been out of bounds to local children, but before long they were seemingly allowed to roam at will. Many accounts bear witness to this security loophole. This was not the case at all bases of course, but certainly where the need for security was minimal there appears to have been a policy of tolerance.

Cadging in

At Warminster in Wiltshire, David Dodge recalls how the local lads cadged in with 'Got any gum chum?' and experienced the delights of Hershey bars. They collected cigar-bands discarded from the cigars that the affluent Americans smoked, and would go behind the Regal Cinema where the floor sweepings were dumped to scavenge for them. Quite often they would also find coins that had been dropped in the dark while films were being shown.

The Americans took over several buildings in Warminster, such as the rear of *The Bath Arms*, some buildings in Ash Walk, and Craven House in Silver Street. The Military Police operated from a shop next to the *Old Bell* in the Market Place. David, his brother and friends would 'cadge fags from the Americans'. They would also roam around Warminster looking for any other discarded items, sometimes even coming home with blankets.

On one occasion, on a piece of land called Copheap, his brother and friends found the complete kit and personal belongings of a soldier who had quite evidently deserted. 'My brother brought all this home in one of our old prams,' he explains, 'and our father went bananas. He went straight up to the MPs office and reported it; he hoped my brother would be punished for theft. The MPs took a note of the incident, and said they would come down and collect the kit – even after several reminders they never did! So we kids gained two genuine American helmets to play with. We still had the soldier's bible (a present from his aunt) several years later. The Military Police would patrol the town in white helmets, with pistols in holsters, swinging their truncheons casually; we kids kept our distance.'

For children in particular with an eye for business, there was brass to be made from the Yanks.

Jean Angel, who was five years old when war was declared, lived in Great Yeldham, about one-and-a-half miles from the airbase of the 381st Bomb Group at Ridgewell. She can remember lorries going through the village, both day and night, loaded high with gravel as the runways and

135 'Got any gum chum?' no doubt the two boys are asking in the foreground of this painting, which shows the Super Sixth lined up in the Gloucestershire town of Moreton-in-Marsh. (Reproduced from a postcard: painting by Ken Aitken and reproduced with the permission of Gerry Tyack/Wellington Aviation Museum)

136 Raymond and Ken (on bike) Perham, in front of the fire station at the American Army hospital in Axminster. (Photo: courtesy of Sheila Pitman)

base were being constructed. With few entertainment facilities available for the men, a big barn was converted into a canteen and club, which also attracted the inevitable camp followers, with whom Jean says her mother was very disgusted but admits, 'We could never understand why'. The club was opposite an orchard next to her house, from which her oldest brother would collect all the beer mugs. He would return these to the club, receiving a penny for each. She also remembers that, even before breakfast, he would walk the length of the High Street to pick up any loose change that the men had dropped or thrown away. Being a good son, he would then present this cache to his mother.

Sometimes cadging in had a tendency to back-fire on local children, and no doubt fed up with the constant pestering GIs were known to play the odd trick or two. A good example of which was when, as a lad, Mr K. Grimes was returning home from Priory School in Taunton. His route took him past two Nissen huts, in what is now the Priory car park. These huts were cookhouses and, as he passed, one of the GIs yelled out of a window, 'Hey kid! Want some chocolate?' The man's unsuspecting victim eagerly ran up to the window, where he was handed a jumbo-sized brown bar, from which he immediately took a huge bite.

'My joy at this unexpected treat,' he explains, 'took an instant nose-dive as the taste of GI soap, laundry variety, hit my taste-buds. With a yell of "lousy bum!" I pitched a neat curve with my bar of chocolate, through the open window and in amongst the group of laughing GIs inside. The baseball players amongst them couldn't have failed to be impressed.'

Of course, young boys are always on the lookout for cigarettes, and many of the Yanks smoked cigars, much stronger than anything they had previously scrounged. Near the GI camps around Truro, such as the one at Malpas Park, there were notices that read, 'Civilians are forbidden to loiter, or talk to troops.' But this didn't stop the young Bernard Peters and his gang from pestering the Yanks. The sentries on duty at Malpas Park would chat to the kids when they were bored; 'Besides,' says Bernard, 'they could see we were just schoolboys.' He recalls following one Yank down Malpas Road as he smoked a big cigar. Before he got to the camp entrance he threw it to one side, where it rolled over the pavement edge dropping down on to the sandy shingle of the river. The tide was out, so one of the gang, Batty, jumped down and retrieved the half-finished cigar butt: they then walked up past the camp, taking turns to have a puff. When they got to Sunny Corner they climbed on top of the swimming hut, hiding away to smoke some Woodbines which Dinky had got from a cigarette machine. In those days they were five for 2d. Sitting astride the roof of the changing hut, Fuzzy persisted in smoking the cigar butt, until it made him so dizzy that he fell off onto the concrete floor below.

Bryan White who lived in Underhill on Portland throughout the war recalls that the huge food dump the Americans built at Castletown led to a bit of bother for a few local lads. This food dump was created to feed the invasion force passing through and the Americans stationed locally. There was a tremendous amount of food stored in boxes in a vast area encircled by barbed wire and patrolling guards. This was seen as a challenge by local youngsters and several gangs were involved in raiding it. This went on for some time until eventually someone was caught and in fear he gave every name he could think of. The following day several high-ranking American officers attended the school, and interviewed every boy on their list.

Lorries visited each of their addresses and collected all the stolen rations they could. When all of the evidence was stacked up in the court, one could barely see the magistrate. Luckily for the boys, the Americans chose not to pursue the case with evil intent and, although one or two had probation, the majority were let off with a stern talking to.

As an eight-year-old, John Matthews, who lived in Poole in Dorset, was quite an entrepreneur. He was already doing a newspaper delivery round to many houses in the area, when suddenly Americans were billeted in several of these properties, including a hall and house in Jolliffe Road, and a larger house in Fernside Road. The Americans he found there were keen to buy a daily paper, and Mr Bland the owner of the newsagent's was quite happy to supply him with extra copies, when he daily arrived at 6a.m. to begin his round.

'From then on,' he says, 'it was a daily visit to these soldiers who were away from home and lonely. They were especially lonely for female company and I was regularly asked if I had sisters, and was given chewing gum and ration packs to bribe me into bringing my two sisters down. My parents, similar to all the other parents in the area, frowned on their daughters having any contact with the Americans, or any service personnel for that matter, so there was a continual, "I'll bring them down" which never materialised.'

John's visits continued on a daily basis and he became the proud possessor of American comics, such as editions of *Superman* and *Batman*, which once read, could be used as swapping currency at school. His other employment consisted of the delivery of groceries after school and chipping chips by hand in the local fish and chip shop in the evening. Here he would again see his American friends, who were all very partial to fish and chips.

'In those days,' he explains, 'a portion of fish and chips cost one shilling and sixpence and they would pay with either a two shilling piece or half a crown. Quite often they would tell the proprietor to "give the change to John".'

John Owen provided a valuable service to the men at the Burtonwood airbase near Warrington, by using his mother's pram to ferry between 30 and 40 portions of cod and chips to the guards on duty. For this service he would be paid 6d. or sometimes a shilling, plus of course a free portion of cod and chips into the bargain. 'Warrington became a very wealthy community,' he points out, 'through a massive input of spending power. Initial resentment blended into a warm and welcoming gratitude to these young guys, who at the end of the day had come to fight with us.'

Rosemary Farrow was only nine when the aerodrome at Raydon in Suffolk was built. There was no chance of wandering around the operational airfield itself, but the living quarters for the airmen and a hospital were built in the nearby village of Great Wenham where she lived, and here it was quite a different story. 'They brought most material by train,' Rosemary recalls, 'using the railway which had been out of use for a number of years.'

However, the American lorries turned the village roads into quagmires, and the visitors felt obliged to ferry the children daily to school at Capel St Mary. 'So we benefited almost immediately,' Rosemary notes. 'Along with the trucks came candy and an interest in our little school. In return we were taught several American patriotic songs and Stephen Foster melodies by our head mistress. In fact we were always around at four in the afternoon when the American national anthem was played over the loud-speakers of the camp, and we joined in and saluted the flag!'

The school children were not actually allowed in the living quarters themselves, or the hospital, but were at liberty to roam around the canteen, the PX club and the cinema, called The Thunderbolt Theatre. Rosemary has fond memories of seeing Bob Hope entertaining troops from the back of a truck, but admits that she was never permitted to watch any of the stage shows put on in the Thunderbolt – 'too "blue", I suppose', she suggests.

Appropriately, the living quarters at Great Wenham were given names like Dodge City, Youngertown, Powder River, and Greenwich Village, while the guardroom was christened Alcatraz. They also had a small chapel, at which villagers were very welcome, although several men from the camp would regularly attend services at the Gospel chapel in the village as well.

At Tibenham in Norfolk, Dorothy Knapp says that one of her brothers virtually lived at the American camp at weekends, similar to many other local boys. 'They were quite safe with the Americans,' she points out. 'In fact, the only time he got it wrong is when he came home with a crewcut. Mum was not happy.' Dorothy's brother and his friends would line up with the soldiers at chow time, and were given a share of their food to eat.

She clearly remembers one of the not so auspicious occasions, when she visited the camp herself. The children only had one bicycle among three of them, and on the morning in question they all balanced

137 Bob Hope goes through the finer points of baseball with Colonel Marion and Captain Southworth during his visit to the 303rd in July 1943. (Photo: courtesy of Mark Forlow)

precariously on it: one on the pedals, another on the seat and the third on the carrier. 'Of course we had to pass the sentry box,' Dorothy reveals. 'The MP stepped out into middle of the road to check a Jeep and my sister decided to steer between the sentry box and the MP. He stepped back and we knocked him over. I can remember his white helmet rolling across the road. We said we were very sorry and went on our way. No one was hurt.'

Some of the ladies in the village did washing for the GIs and occasionally Dorothy would accompany an older friend as she was returning it. They had to go into the accommodation huts to deliver the laundry, where the men would be sitting on their beds. 'We were quite safe,' she reiterates. 'They always asked if we had a big sister at home.'

At Broadstone in Dorset, part of the US 1st Infantry Division's Services of Supply requisitioned several properties. Roy Stevens and his friends were prone to making camps at the bottom of one of these and in time got to know the soldiers very well. They would often be welcomed into the living accommodation. The clubhouse of what had been Broadstone Golf Club became the Officers Mess, and Roy and his companions would shamelessly rummage in the kitchen dustbins to see what would surface. At a time of civil deprivation he likens the dustbins at the American Officers Mess to a veritable treasure trove, as they yielded up their cache of unopened cans of orange juice or spaghetti.

One of the village shops was taken over by the PX club and store, where once a week the GIs could draw out their allocation of cigarettes: notably Camel, Lucky Strike, or Chesterfield. They also had an allocation of chocolate and other sweets, which the Americans put under the general heading of 'candy'. Roy remembers chocolate bars such as Babe

Ruth and Hershey bars, and of course Juicy Fruit and other brands of chewing gum. Well, as you can imagine, on the appointed day the local lads would lay siege to the store and waylay any emerging Yanks laden down with their goodies. Understandably, the soldiers soon got tired of the constant pestering, and hit on what Ray called 'a particularly ingenious idea'. Each soldier adopted one of the boys and would only give his candy to his particular 'chosen one'. Roy's own benefactor was a 'tall, mustachioed Top Sergeant from Texas'.

Enrico Cortese who describes himself as Italo-American admits that he was 'one of those many Yanks who were overpaid, oversexed, and over there'. The only problem is, he furthers, 'In fact I was in Yeovil, lonely and sick at heart'.

That was until he met a local boy called Derek Berkley. Enrico was billeted in the gymnasium of a public school and was lying on a mattress cover filled with hay, when a group of cocky ten-year-olds came in, asking, 'Got any gum chum?'

One boy he remembers was too shy to enter, staying instead by the doorway with a running nose. Enrico held out some candy and said, 'Come and get it kid!' The young lad shook his head from side to side and stayed firmly where he was. Not to be defeated, Enrico raised himself and walked across to the boy to hand him the goodies. A smile appeared, and after that Enrico and Derek became good friends. The lad would visit the gym each day, and Enrico would ask the mess sergeant to completely fill his mess set due to his large appetite: of course he then shared the food with his new companion.

In time, Enrico was introduced to Derek's mum Vera who befriended him like a sister and, during the remainder of his stay and before moving on to a camp in Honiton, life was at least bearable thanks to a family from Somerset. Derek sadly passed away quite young, and Enrico says, 'I often think of my little friend who made life a bit more livable, and it fills my heart with hope that the children of today will not mess up this world as my generation did!'

A DANGEROUS PLAYGROUND

For children in the area, having an operational airbase on their doorstep was hugely exciting. Bryan Potter recalls how he and his pals would walk the three miles from Bury St Edmunds to the airbase at Rougham. They would cut across fields to arrive at the huge mounds of raised earth around the perimeter of the base. Lying down, they would then wait for the B-17s to return from their raids, and watch as they taxied to their hard standings before firing off any spare ammunition from their guns. 'Sounds dangerous,' he admits, 'and I guess we shouldn't have been there.'

Sometimes, if noticed by staff at the base, they would be ordered away. But occasionally, if they were spotted by one of the aircraft crews, they would be called over to the fence and given wax boxes of sweets and chocolate. This surely made the dangers pale into insignificance.

'On the way back,' he continues, 'we would pick up any spent machine-gun ammunition cases that were lying around.' He claims that his grandfather was a 'wiz' in his cellar workshop and would use his ingenuity and soldering iron to turn the spent cartridges into table lighters. Some of the Americans were so impressed by his craftsmanship, that they would beg to buy them as wartime souvenirs.

When in 1943 an American base was built at Earls Colne for the 323rd Bomb Group, 9th USAAF, the children from nearby Eight Ash Green, including Geoffrey Charge, would cycle over to watch the aircraft leaving and returning on their daylight bombing missions. These were B-26 Marauder bombers with their fighter escort of either Thunderbolts or Mustangs. There was a hedge around the perimeter of the base, and on one occasion the boys found a hole which they crept through. On the other side they discovered a couple of fuel drop-tanks, which he admits to stealing, dragging back through the hedge, and wheeling home on their bicycles. These fuel tanks were made into canoes and launched on the local river, but they were only used once or twice before the village policeman found out and lectured them about how dangerous they were. So on the following evening, the boys took them back to the base and, unobserved, pushed them back through the hole in the hedge.

One problem faced by the Americans was how to dispose of their rubbish. Ron Green lived on the border of Wymondham and Crownthorpe in Norfolk and had to take Chapel Lane into Wymondham each day to school. On this lane were two large dry gravel pits. The deepest of these was about 30 feet and at the far side, in the steepest edge, there was (he recalls) a colony of nesting sand martins. The ambition of the local children was to collect their eggs. Egg collecting, although illegal now, was a popular hobby with young boys in the 1940s. The children would

138 A busy scene at Rougham. For children, living near an operational base was hugely exciting, but also presented many dangers. Bryan Potter lived three miles from Rougham, the airfield depicted in this painting by Joe Crowfoot. (Reproduced with the permission of Joe Crowfoot)

either try to reach down from the top of the cliff edge, or would stand on each others' shoulders at its bottom and try to reach up, although Ron has to concede defeat, admitting that they never actually managed to acquire any of the eggs.

Every day, he explains, a lorry would turn up 'with junk from the airfields', at the same time as the kids were making their way to school. They would ask the drivers for gum, or chocolate, and Ron recalls asking for 'Yankee comics with Superman fighting his enemy Doctor Carver'.

When the lorries had gone, the children would climb into the pit, hunting for anything they could exchange with their friends at school. Airplane glass, in particular, was a valuable commodity which came from the canopy of cockpits and windows of the Flying Fortresses. 'It was a kind of perspex,' Ron describes, 'clear and about four millimeters thick.'

One day he stumbled on quite a large piece of this perspex, making him late for school again, the usual punishment for which was the cane, especially for the older boys. The piece he found was about 14 by 16 inches in size, and he notes that the boys would normally cut a smaller piece off such a big bit, usually about the size of a modern 50 pence coin. Then with the army knives that most boys possessed, they would proceed to make a hole in the middle, producing a ring big enough to fit the finger of their girlfriend.

'Well this big bit I found,' explains Ron, 'I got it to school but as I didn't have my dad's hacksaw there, I proceeded to make the hole first, and by break time I had this done under the school desk. I was nine then and had met the loveliest eight-year-old. She was keen to try this ring on although it was surrounded on three sides by about 14 inches of spare perspex. Well as you can surmise, it stuck fast. I took her to the boys' wash room, found a bit of soap but it didn't work. She cried, so we went to the girls' toilet, but got caught by a most cold-hearted woman teacher and she was carted off. I found myself with a tall dunce's hat placed on my head for a time, standing in the corner of the classroom. At home time I went to the headmistress's room, knocked on the door and said, "Please, Miss, can I have my bit of airplane glass back?". Well I got something alright, that was my second mistake that day.'

Ron and his friends would sometimes come to school with bandoleers of used cartridges, and occasionally live ones. Many large bomb boxes would also be thrown into these pits, which were ideal for rabbit hutches, even though it was quite a struggle to get them to the top of the steep slopes. What was even more frustrating, was to have them taken off you by ladies from Wicklewood, who would push prams to the site in order to take home large quantities of discarded trash. The only chance you had against the Wicklewood mums, was if your own mother was at hand to protect you. Most of the men folk were, of course, away in the army.

Ron recalls that, when the Yanks left in 1945, one of the pits was almost completely full of tin cans. He saw his chance, at last, of reaching the sand martin colony. He began to walk across the cans, until he found himself being sucked down into a quicksand of tin. At

139 Munitions store Wendling. Such stock-piles could be found all over East Anglia, which naturally posed a danger to the neighbouring communities. (Photo: courtesy of www.b24. net)

about six feet from the edge he was waist deep in rubbish, but managed to crawl back to safety.

'The poor sand martins finally lost their nesting site,' he continues, 'when soil was placed over the top of the pit.' Today several houses have been built on the area, quite oblivious to the fact that beneath them lie 30 feet of tin cans, live ammunition, and who knows what else.

As a boy Ron kept a pet jackdaw, which he once sold to an American for two shillings, only to have the bird fly home again. Jackdaws weren't ideal pets because they have a tendency to take shiny things, and in turn the bird flew off and lost two shillings of his money. He explains that many birds, such as crows, blackbirds, and especially jackdaws, had reason to thank the Yanks for nest-building material. To confuse German radar the Americans took silver paper on their missions, and quite often on the return journey this would be thrown out of the aircraft before landing. These silver strips would attract the jackdaws who would fly off with the paper and stuff it into the hollows of old English trees, or hawthorn bushes, adorning them like Christmas trees.

John Peck, who lived in Gloucester during the war years, can remember an American landfill site on the Severn flood plain, not far from his garden. 'This was used by the American forces,' he explains, 'to dump vast quantities of material. Nobody knows exactly what was dumped, but we gleaned from the heap enormous amounts of wooden packing cases, which we used for lighting fires; we also found huge tins of Spam and so on, which nobody had the courage to consume in case they were in some way contaminated.'

Some people suggested that entire vehicles were dumped in this landfill site, but the truth will never be known as it has now been redeveloped as a retail park. John remembers watching as the pile drivers sliced down through the soil, thinking to himself of the layers of American rubbish below.

Dave Ford and his mates, who grew up at Underhill on the island of Portland, were always scrounging to find anything of use that the American Naval personnel billeted at Castletown threw into 44-gallon drums. This became a frequent after-school activity and Saturday exploration. 'Soon every boy sported a doughboy hat,' he claims. 'A useful bargaining possession to swap for another's goods if fancied.'

In these waste drums one was likely to find American field K rations; in them there were cigarettes – a prized possession of any boy who was learning to smoke – a packet of four dry biscuits, hard boiled sweets and a tin of processed meat. Another prized possession was an inflatable life belt, with which many children learned to swim.

'Further collectors items,' he lists, 'were the stamps from envelopes, cigar bands and chewing gum wrappers, all of which were stuck in a school exercise book and the many, many different cigar bands looked very colourful. I remember a classmate who lived in Castletown, John Smythe, and had a very good collection of cigar bands.'

Some of the older boys would find discarded live ammunition, even cannon shells, from which the shell could be prised off to empty out the cordite to make a firework. Some boys discovered that you could easily prise the shell off by inserting it into the hole of a railway line. 'Unfortunately,' Dave explains, 'some boys were injured when one exploded.'

Derek Chorley, who was a pupil at the Royal Caledonian Schools, Bushey, very near to HQ 8th USAAF Fighter Command, remembers that a lot of infantry training went on in the area. One day, one of the pupils found a live round of ammunition. He managed to take off the cartridge case and struck a match near the gunpowder, which blew up in his face. The boy was badly burnt and had to be rushed to hospital, where thankfully he made a full recovery from his burns.

Similarly at Tiverton in Devon, Geoff Grater recalls that, when the troops left for D-Day, they were rather careless in leaving bullet cases, badges and other ephemera lying about, which became a great source of swapping trade amongst the kids in his road. One of his friends clamped a bullet in the vice in their garden shed and hit the base of it with a nail and hammer in the hope that it would go off. 'Fortunately it did not,' he says with relief, 'as it would have smashed the glass window in our shed.'

Geoff also remembers an occasion when he crept up behind an American soldier who was strolling down their road with a rifle slung over his shoulder. The boy fired his cap pistol at the young man and cried 'Bang, you're dead!' The GI swung quickly around, taking hold of his rifle as he did so, and then proceeded to point its muzzle at the head of the boy behind him. 'I thought he was going to blow my head off,' states Geoff. Then, after what seemed an eternity, the man lowered his rifle and said, 'You were nearly a dead man. Never point a gun at anyone, even if it is a toy.' Geoff was only six years old at the time, but learned a very valuable lesson.

PARTIES AND PRESENTS

During the war years, Gladys Fellingham was living at a children's home near the American airbase at Rattlesden in Suffolk, which was the home of the 447th Bomb Group, with their B-17s. Young airmen from the base would regularly visit the home and play games with the children. Sometimes they would bring instruments to entertain them, and in the winter months an entire band would arrive. They would also bring them sweets and chocolate, and other things that weren't available in Britain at the time. They would throw parties on the base and invite the children from the orphanage to attend. She has particularly fond memories of the Christmas party they gave for the orphanage children in 1944, where there was even ice-cream on the menu. Many of the young servicemen weren't much older than some of the children themselves and Gladys kept in touch with two pen pals for several years after the war.

Rosemary Allen, who was born in Swaffham in Norfolk at the beginning of 1938, also remembers how the Americans treated the local children to a party at their base at North Pickenham, about three miles from her house. This was the home of both 492nd Bomb Group, and 491st Bomb Group, with their B-24s. She thinks the party in question was held at Christmas in 1943, when she was nearly six years old.

All the schoolchildren from Swaffham were invited to attend the party, and transport in the form of army trucks arrived at the market place to pick them up. Filled with excitement, the children clambered into the back of these sturdy vehicles and were driven the short distance to the base, where they were initially shepherded into the dining hall and seated for a meal. And what a meal it was! For the first course there was turkey with all the trimmings and, as Rosemary had been used to rationing for most of her young life, this plentiful and rich food made her feel a little sick about half way through the feast.

'Someone must have told the young American who was looking after our table,' she says, 'because he took me by the hand and led me off to the toilets. I wasn't sick – it was just excitement and indigestion from the rich food that I wasn't used to – but he patiently waited for me, and then took me back to my table where I thoroughly enjoyed the fruit salad that followed.'

Following the meal the children enjoyed a cartoon show, before being chauffeured home again. During this journey Rosemary and her friend Margaret were privileged to find themselves travelling in the vehicle's cab, with the driver who kindly left them both with a supply of chewing gum! 'We all had a really good time,' she recalls, 'and, looking back, it was a wonderful gesture from the Americans to bring such happiness into our rather austere young lives.'

Bryan Potter recalls that the American airmen had a social club in Southgate Street, Bury St Edmunds, where he lived. Bury was quite a busy place at the time, being the base of the 4th Combat Wing, and just a few miles out of town was the Rougham airbase. He also recalls how at Christmas the Americans would organise a party for local children. 'At a time when chocolate, ice-cream, sweets and toys were scarce, those parties had everything,' he says, 'and there was a great bonding with grateful local parents.'

Similarly, at the aerodrome at Eye in Suffolk, the Americans put on a Christmas party for the local kids, at which Joy Matthews was introduced to 'chocolate beans' for the first time: 'Smarties' in plain English. She also remembers trying to eat ice-cream with a fork, which must have been a messy experience. For many of the children, this would have been their first encounter with such delights. 'It was so warm in that hut,' she says, 'we thought we'd died and gone to heaven.'

Walter Perry recalls the Christmas party that was given at the aerodrome at Ridgewell in 1943, near where his parents ran a country pub. 'We were collected by truck, and two or three Americans acted as "uncles" to us children, seeing we had a good time and returned us to our homes at the end of the festivities. Spam sandwiches, jellies, ice-creams and the like we had not had for some

140   Private First Class Louie Braden of New Orleans. While serving at Wattisham in Suffolk he was a welcome visitor at the home of Sylvia Patching's uncle and aunt in the village of Bricett. Her uncle worked on the airfield. Private Braden wrote the following note in Sylvia's autograph book, dated 25 June 1944: 'When skies are cloudy, remember behind those clouds is the sun. So is life. Remember a Yank.' (Photo: courtesy of Sylvia Patching)

time. Entertainment by conjurors, clowns, games with small prizes and a sing-along made it a magical afternoon, finally capped with a small packet of sweets to take home. Sadly, for the fortunate few it was not repeated, not because we misbehaved, but it was unfair for children who lived just outside the designated area, or were just over the age limit, so it became unmanageable.'

Jean Angel, who lived at Great Yeldham in Essex, also went to the Christmas party at Ridgewell, but recalls there being a Santa Claus giving every child a present. Similarly, Dorothy Knapp recalls there being a Father Christmas at the wonderful parties held at Tibenham in Norfolk. The children would be picked up from school in two army lorries.

Sylvia Patching, who came from Ipswich, found herself performing at one of these parties. She had relatives living in the village of Great Bricett, which is just down the road from the Wattisham Aerodrome. Her uncle worked on the airfield and he and her aunt befriended one of the GIs. His name was PFC Louie Braden and, if he got frustrated, one of his sayings was, 'Oh! My aching back!'

'One Christmas,' Sylvia explains, 'I was in a play written by a couple from the "big house" at Bricett, entitled *The Children's Dream.*

Consequence of this was that we were asked to perform it again at the drome where a party was organised for local children. We were picked up by lorry and transported to the base. After the party we were all given presents. Don't remember what mine consisted of except for a memo book. Dark brown cover which I made into an address book and still have it.'

But these Christmas parties weren't only held at airfields. At Broadstone in Dorset, Roy Stevens went to a 'slap-up party' for all the children held at the Women's Institute. Afterwards they were given rides around the Dorset countryside in Jeeps. 'I remember hanging on for dear life,' says Roy, 'as our driver careered around Broadstone at breakneck speed!'

And of course, not all parties were held at Christmas. Mr R.E. Bennett recalls a party thrown at Great Ashfield in Suffolk, which was put on to celebrate the base having done two hundred missions. At this party a stage was erected in one of the hangars, and The Glenn Miller Band, and he thinks, Bing Crosby, Bob Hope, and others were there to entertain.

At the Christmas party staged on the airfield at Boreham in Essex, the entertainment was provided by the GIs themselves. One of those attending was Colin Sarel, who recalls how all the children from the village Church of England school were invited, and ferried to the airfield in 'large left-hand drive personnel carriers'. They were treated to plates of sandwiches and jelly, and Colin tasted ice-cream for the very first time. The airmen staged a show for the children, singing Christmas carols and popular melodies of the time. This party also whetted Colin's appetite for electronic organs, as the music was provided by a very early Hammond Organ, making it, in his opinion, 'a truly memorable event'.

A feast of a different kind was enjoyed by a young Anita O'Brien and a group of her friends, who had travelled by train from Horfield Station in Bristol to Severn Beach for the day. 'After a visit to the funfair and then probably the Blue Lagoon,' she reflects, 'we walked along the path towards the boating lake. Looking down on the green between the path and a row of shops we noticed Yanks assembling tables. We sat down on the grass slope and watched, as all sorts of food was laid out and there was the tantalizing smell of sausages and onions filling our noses.'

141 Carole Miller outside her Taunton home in June 1948, with the doll sent to her from Al Johnson in Milwaukee. (Photo: courtesy of Carole Miller)

142 Two airmen enjoy the entertainment with local children at the camp theatre at Molesworth, during the 1943 Children's Christmas Party. The vicar in the second row looks suitably amused. (Photo: courtesy of Mark Forlow)

Basically, the Americans were treating their English girlfriends to a barbecue, which was something quite new to the British. Anita remembers how all the cooks wore white hats as they served food to the waiting throng. Suddenly, on noticing their audience on the grass bank, the Yanks called out to the children inviting them to come and join them. 'At the end of our feast,' says Anita, 'we were told to help ourselves to oranges, the likes of which we hadn't seen for a long while. So clutching about four each, we made our way back to the train station and home.'

Carole Miller was only a baby during the war, but her parents Nancy and Bill Brown often told her about their American friend from Milwaukee, Al Johnson, who would visit their home in Alfred Street, Taunton, which was near Victoria Park, where some of the Americans were billeted. After he had returned to the States, the family received many letters from Al. Then one day in 1948, when she was six years old, there was a parcel waiting for her, on her return from the Priory School. The parcel was addressed to her personally and inside was a beautiful doll with closing eyes, which was really lovely. She still has the doll today and the customs declaration for five dollars. Her mother received the biggest box of goodies in the post, containing many things that were still rationed in England. Really precious things like cotton, needles, material, buttons, lipstick, sweets, toiletries, and other things that Carole can no longer remember. This was by way of a big 'thank you' to the Browns for befriending him.

Sheila Stacey was four years old when D-Day took place and lived in Long Copse, Holbury. She clearly remembers the American soldiers being camped beside their house for several days. Her parents welcomed them into their home, and offered to do their washing for them. In return, the grateful soldiers brought cigarettes, sweets, and nylons. She believes her grandfather was even given several cans of petrol, which was a particular bonus at a time of severe rationing.

One soldier called Norman was very kind to the young Sheila, even teaching her to ride her bicycle. He promised to write to the family

143 Santa makes a welcome appearance at Molesworth, during a Christmas Party for local children on 24 December 1943. (Photo: courtesy of 303rd Bomb Group Association)

from France, and kept his promise. But more than that, he arranged for his mother in America to send Sheila a parcel. 'I don't think I had ever received a parcel through the post before,' she states. She opened it with excitement to discover inside all manner of wonderful things, including sweets, chewing gum and two dolls. 'I still have one of the dolls today,' says Sheila. She named the doll Joan, because, as far as she remembers, either Norman's mother or sister was called Joan.

Ann Morley's gift was a doll's cradle, made for her by a special GI friend called Freddie. When she was seven or eight, her aunt and uncle managed a public house on the A46 between Stroud and Bath. It was then called *The Black Horse*, but is today known as the *Tippotts Inn*. Americans were based nearby and would come into the pub for drinks. So whenever Ann visited her aunt and uncle, she came away with a good supply of chewing gum and candy, which suddenly made her a very popular girl at school.

144 Is it a bird, is it a plane, or is it Santa Claus? In this picture taken during the 1943 Children's Christmas Party at Molesworth, an American points to something in the sky. (Photo: courtesy of Mark Forlow)

Some of the Americans eventually found their way to her parents' house, where her mother and father proved very hospitable and welcoming. Ann particularly remembers one young soldier she thinks was called Freddie Lequer and, although she was very young at the time and it is now a distant memory, she believes it was Freddie who made the dolls' cradle. Making a gift of such magnitude seems so caring and sensitive, at a time when this young soldier must surely have felt concerned for his future. Ann still has the cradle and says, 'I expect one day I shall pass it on to my granddaughter but feel she won't have the same thoughts about it as I do myself.'

Chapter 10

Bolero and Beyond

In the early months of 1944, much of England's West Country began to fill with camps and troops, as *Operation Bolero*, the preparation for D-Day, continued in earnest. The code word 'Bolero' had been used for this massive build-up of men and materials because, similar to Ravel's musical composition of the same name, it would begin on a small, gentle scale, steadily growing to a triumphant crescendo.

On D-Day itself 55,000 American troops landed on the beaches of Normandy, embarking from ports and harbours all along the south coast of England, from Southampton to Dartmouth. A further 16,000 airborne troops landed by parachute or glider. All of these men fell under the command of the American First Army. Most of them were split into three divisions, the 1st Division, known as the 'Big Red One;' the 4th Division; and the 29th Division, who were famously composed of men from both Maryland and Virginia, opposing sides in the Civil War. Because of this they were known as the 'Blue and Gray,' a name which was reflected in their shoulder patch. Hardly a town or village throughout the West Country didn't feel the effect of this influx of troops in some way. In the final days these three divisions generally descended on the counties of Dorset (1st Division); Devon (4th Division); and Cornwall (29th Division), with some elements of the invasion force spilling over into south Somerset and Hampshire.

How the West was Won

Graham Toms was an 11-year-old living in Eastland Road, Yeovil, when thousands of American troops descended on the town and the surrounding area in February 1944. At least one site at Houndstone Camp had been previously prepared as early as 1942 by black troops of the labour battalions. These were followed by artillery units, infantry, and administrative sections in 1944.

However, the prepared accommodation still wasn't sufficient to house everyone, and men were dispersed around the town, sleeping in schools, private houses, pubs, lofts, skittle alleys, shops, and anywhere else there was available space. The vehicles and artillery were kept at Barwick Park, just south of the town.

'The kids of the town were very impressed with these men with different accents to us,' notes Graham. 'They were billeted all over the town – in fact anywhere there was space to accommodate them – and the general public had their wartime diet supplemented by the extra food the troops gave to them. The Americans helped the schools, gave parties for the kids and were always a good source of candy bars and chewing gum.' They even offered to level-off Yeovil Town Football Club's famously sloping pitch at Huish. It never actually happened and today the club plays at a different location.

There were several mess halls dotted about the town and Graham Toms recalls tasting his first hamburger from the cookhouse in Sherborne Road. 'Kids would hang about to see if there was anything left after the soldiers had finished their meals. I had my first doughnut with a hole in the middle from one of the "Donut Dugouts" that were in town.'

Colin Osborne first encountered the men of the 29th US Infantry Division, when he was an eight- or nine-year-old evacuee in Merriott, Somerset, where he had gone to stay with his grandmother.

G Company of the 11-115 Infantry Regiment, 29th Infantry Division moved into Hamlyn's Store in Lower Street, Merriott, some time in 1943. Colin became particularly friendly with Private First Class William Breece Joines, who was from Kentucky, and he would spend as much time as possible at his billet.

His enduring memory of those troopers was watching them trudge to the Tithe Barn, which was being used as the cook-house, to get their chow, walking through the rain in ponchos with mess tins at the low port. 'How they hated Brussel Sprouts,' he states.

The kids at the village school 'pitched up' with all manner of US Army equipment, including a Colt 45 automatic and complete boxes of K rations, which were available in exchange for a two-day-old copy of the *Daily Express*. He was quite taken aback when one GI he had

145 Members of the 430th Anti-Aircraft Artillery Automatic Weapons Battalion (Mobile), who were based around Yeovil before the invasion. (Photo: courtesy of Graham Toms)

approached for gum asked him whether he 'hated Niggers'. Colin said he didn't and the man's reply was: 'No gum until you become a Nigger hater.'

The story of one young American who struck up a life-long friendship with the Gloucestershire town of Minchinhampton was first told by Stan Dyer, who was later the town's correspondent for the *Citizen* newspaper. He told of how the Americans arrived on the edge of his town in early 1944 and set up camp in the Great Park. Among them were soldiers of the 38th Engineers Regiment, who maintained most of the heavy equipment needed for future operations. They were there to re-organise and re-equip after fighting in North Africa and in preparation for the invasion of France. The camp that quickly appeared consisted of huts, tents and hurriedly constructed roadways, and was fenced off from the public.

146 Bernie De Primo (left) and Jim Ferrell, who passed through Yeovil with the 430th AAAAw Battalion in 1944. Since the end of the war Bernie has returned to Yeovil on a couple of occasions, and during one trip he was shown the plaque which was unveiled in the borough in December 2004, to commemorate the thousands of American servicemen who were based in the area. (Photo: courtesy of Graham Toms)

One of the American soldiers was 22-year-old Private First Class Phil Berardelli of Pittsburgh, Pennsylvania. One day, Phil was sitting in his Jeep in Bell Lane by the church lych gates, just a few yards from the local primary school, when a young lad who had just come out of school approached. He was nine-year-old Geoffrey Ellis, and the two struck up a conversation. Geoffrey was thrilled when invited to sit in Phil's Jeep beside his new found friend. In return, Geoff invited Phil back to his house to meet his parents.

Phil took the little boy home and thus began what Phil in later years described as, 'Not only a most pleasant association but a long-standing one. My memories of the family, and of their gracious hospitality and caring are very dear to me.' He was also saddened by the fact that such a lovely town as Minchinhampton should be disrupted in this way, but obviously knew it was necessary at the time.

Phil's words came to light when Stan Dyer's memories of his friendship with Geoffrey Ellis were published in the *Gloucester Journal*. One of his friends in Gloucestershire evidently sent Phil a copy of the article and before long he was corresponding with Stan. In these letters Phil also recalled Father Proudman, because he and some of his friends attended Sunday Mass at the Church and Priory of the Annunciation at nearby Woodchester. 'Father Proudman became my friend, who later

147 Private 1st Class Phil Berardelli (left), 38th Engineers Regiment, US Army, with buddy from the same Regiment in Minchinhampton Park, 1944. (Photo: courtesy of Stan Dyer)

148 A smart soldier of the 4th Armored Division poses before his truck in Devizes, Wiltshire. (Photo: courtesy of Elsie Lewis)

became a chaplain in the RAF – a lovely man,' said Phil, who then goes on to report that their stay in Minchinhampton came to an end in early May. 'After a sorrowful farewell to the good people of the town, we made our way down to Cornwall where we rehearsed our amphibious landings and practiced gunnery on the local beaches. We were not far from St Austell. As you know, the day arrived in the first week of June and we were shipped out of Plymouth, our destination being Utah Beach. After securing the beach, the regiment, minus the dead and injured, made their way to Cherbourg, then through Belgium and Holland, the rest is history.'

Obviously Phil survived the war, returning to Pittsburgh and marrying his childhood sweetheart Stella. Phil concluded his letter to Stan by saying, 'Dates and places may fade, but the warmth and friendship of the good people of Minchinhampton so precious during those dark days, will forever remain etched in my mind.'

In 1998, the highlight of the Minchinhampton bi-annual Country Fayre was a visit in person by Phil Berardelli and his wife, along with his friend Geoff Ellis and his wife Joy, who now live in Kent. 'I still have a one dollar piece in a presentation box,' writes Stan Dyer, 'given to me by Phil on his return visit to Minch, which was produced by the US government as a souvenir of the 50th anniversary of the end of the war in Europe in 1995.' Sadly, Phil died in 2003 aged 82 and his wife Stella about a year later.

At Fairford in Gloucestershire, when vehicles lined the streets in the weeks before D-Day, or were parked at the US camp in Fairford

149 Men of the 4th Armored Division (Finance Group) relaxing before the invasion. (Photo: courtesy of Elsie Lewis)

Park, the local people couldn't escape noticing what the crews were doing. Crossing the road to the bakery to get the morning buns, Jim Jefferes would see men welding or assembling different things. He got to know one of these men, Sergeant Charles Zimmerself from Chicago, and wrote to his niece Sylvia, who sent him American magazines to read, of which he states, 'These magazines shouted out the prosperity and impressiveness of the USA. They were colourful and well printed on high-class paper, far different than the wartime paper to which we had become accustomed. The pages were filled with American war manufacture, planes, ships, armour and technical developments. One could only be awestruck by the country's enormous manufacturing capacity.'

In May 1944, all the armour disappeared from the town overnight, on its way to the south coast, leaving a marked and ominous stillness. The aircraft at Fairford airbase were being painted with large white bands, which today we know were their invasion livery, to ease identification. Gliders were being prepared by the hundred.

In September or October 1943 Jim Timoney recalls the scene at Beaminster in Dorset, when elements of the American First Infantry Division rolled into town. The cannon company and the anti-tank company of the 16th Infantry Regiment were billeted all over the town in requisitioned properties, with the town square itself being used as the parade ground with a flag-raising and lowering ceremony each day. Parnham House, just to the south of the town, became the headquarters of the 16th Infantry and many rumours abounded of the various generals such as Eisenhower and Montgomery who paid a visit.

A short time later the parkland at Parnham House filled with tanks and the crews slept in tents nearby. Opportunities abounded for the likes of Jim Timoney, who recalls being handed a pound note and asked to get a loaf of bread from Hodges the bakers. The bread cost four pence and he was told to 'keep the change'. The pubs in the town were open for about one night a week, or until the beer ran out, and queues outside the fish and chip shop, where his mother worked, stretched up the road. 'The Americans really took to our fish and chips,' he states. When Military Policemen came into the shop, who were apparently not allowed to queue, they asked his little sister to get their supper, and in return gave her helmet liners full of candy and gum. 'She hoarded this I remember in a large drawer,' says Jim, 'and wouldn't give me any.'

Ivor Strange notes that anyone seeing this massive build-up of arms and supplies around the south of England had a shrewd idea that something very big was coming up. As already described, the huge park at Kingston Maurward House was turned into one massive petrol dump. Fuel cans were stacked in piles of thousands all over the park. The house itself was used to quarter the personnel and there was even a Bofors anti-aircraft gun mounted on the roof.

For residents of south Dorset, May and early June 1944 brought a noticeable movement in troops and equipment. Everything was converging on the south coast and the coastal port areas began to fill to capacity. In every town, or village, or even just along the country roads from Puddletown to Salisbury, or Wimborne to Lyme Regis, vehicles were parked end-to-end: trucks, half-tracks pulling guns, tanks, amphibious vehicles and Jeeps. Their crews either slept in their vehicles or in temporary accommodation nearby.

Suddenly in June 1944, the streets of Dorchester erupted into a continual flow as men and vehicles passed through on their way to Weymouth. From his prime position at the gunshop in East High Street, Ivor could view what appeared to be an endless stream of tanks and trucks, laden with battle-ready GIs, and everywhere 'Snowdrops' in their white helmets and gloves directed the traffic. With a sharp change down through the gears, most of the vehicles turned successfully into South Street, but he recalls that the historic town pump, which had always been there as a source of water during the time of horse-drawn transport, took quite a battering.

150 Rodney Pearce emerging from the entrance to GB Cave on the Mendips in the early 1940s. (Photo: courtesy of Rodney Pearce)

'Another spot on the route to Weymouth which caught out many Yank drivers,' he explains, 'was the bend at Upwey Hill.' More than once, due to break failure or for some other reason, vehicles ploughed through a wall to the valley below, and children and adults alike would quickly gather to witness the scene.

As the build up to D-Day continued, Bernard Peters remembers much of the hard-labouring work done by the black troops in the area around Truro. This was unavoidable because they would be down at their favourite beauty spots on the river Fal, where local people liked to picnic, play, or fish. But now the black GIs were building slipways, and laying the concrete and steel matting on which they assembled landing craft. They also cut through what had been almost virgin land to lay a tarmac road, still there today.

These black GIs were SOS, rather like our own Pioneer Corps and RASC. Some were truck drivers, or boat and port personnel, who helped with the wounded on the D-Day beaches. Others drove the Higgins boat, manned stations on warships, or piloted LSTs (Landing Ship Tank). Several special black brigades were formed, such as the 1st ESB (Engineer Special Brigade), which was with the 4th Infantry Division on Utah Beach: the 5th ESB with the 16th and the 6th ESB with the 116th on Omaha beach. They demolished obstacles, blew up mines, erected guide signs and cleared access roads. They blew gaps in sea walls and put down supplies, ammo dumps, or acted as beach traffic cops. It's amazing that, in the majority of war films, you rarely glimpse a black soldier, but they were evident in their thousands, often doing some of the most unpleasant jobs imaginable.

FINAL DAYS

Colin Osborne, who was staying in Merriott, remembers the final kit lay-out, before the men of the 29th US Infantry Division moved off, for their eventual embarkation for Normandy. On that day, the whole of G Company were turned out into a meadow off Lower Street, where they laid out all their kit. He spent a long time chatting with his friend Bill, until the TCVs arrived to take them to Fowey in Cornwall, from where they 'jumped off' on D-Day, landing on Omaha Beach.

'What I do remember is going back to Hamlyn's Store after G Company had gone,' writes Colin. 'All the beds had been laid out with personal kit to be forwarded to their next of kin, should the worst happen. Some of the items were mouthwateringly luxurious. I admit to stealing a black plastic soap-box that I gave to my dad.'

Colin also remembers a GI called Terry, the company runner, who rode a khaki Harley Davidson. It was Terry who later returned to tell them the extent of the casualties at Omaha Beach. Bill Breece had survived the day, but was killed in action a few months later, the day before the regiment was due to come out of the line for a much earned rest.

Bernard Galpin remembers when the 101st Airborne Division set up camp near Chard in Somerset. 'I remember the US Army camp in Furnham Road well,' he writes, 'and have fond memories of that time.

There was quite a gang of us that frequented the camp. Some of us had passes, as we often ran errands for the troops – especially to the Sunshine Cider Mills for cider. I used to take home clean laundry to be ironed by my mother, mostly shirts. They used to pay her five shillings a time, which was a lot in those days.'

That particular part of the camp he recalls was mostly tented, and hurriedly put up to accommodate the extra troops arriving for D-Day. At the time Bernard was staying with his grandmother at Cuttiford's Door, just a few miles away, so he was able to visit the camp quite often. Prior to D-Day the security was stepped up, but the kids were mostly ignored, only occasionally told to 'Get the hell out of here!' The cookhouse was their favourite haunt as the Yanks were well fed and generous. Again, shortly before D-Day, there was a lot of activity in the camp with the troops having to weigh themselves and their kit, and anything over a certain weight had to be ditched. Bernard remembers large pits being dug, and sacks hanging on posts full of surplus kit. The pits were eventually filled in, and needless to say he acquired a few items.

151   In this picture landing craft are being loaded at Brixham in south Devon, shortly before D-Day. (Photo: courtesy of Alan Heather/Torquay Museum)

'I recall one chap,' he says, 'who was very reluctant to throw away a box of fishing tackle. His mates told him that he would not be needing it where they were going. I often wonder how many of them made it back to the States?'

Chard reservoir was used by engineers to practise bridge building and Bernard also remembers seeing landing craft there as well. 'We used to wonder why they kept putting part of a bridge up and then taking it down again!!'

Another interesting story tells how the Americans were responsible for much of the exploration of Mendip caves after the war. Rodney Pearce, who was an experienced caver and member of the Mendip Cave Rescue Association, took many Americans caving. Prior to D-Day many American units did their final training for the invasion on top of the Mendips. Some of the training, at Rodney Pearce's invitation, included caving from Charterhouse into GB Cave, one of the more difficult descents on the Mendips at that time. Most of the Americans had never been caving before, but they treated the experience as part of their hardening-up process for the invasion. They took it well, including an Apache Indian who went down in moccasins. During one trip, one particularly large soldier got himself stuck in a narrow passage called Buggery Bend. He began to panic, which made matters worse. In the end Rodney Pearce managed to drag him back a few feet and rotate his body. Then, following the application of an acetylene lamp to his backside, he slid through quite easily, when his battle dress began to steam.

The result of all this was that the Americans left behind a lot of stores at the Mendip camp. There was an incredible selection of canned meat, various canned vegetables, beer and whisky, all of which kept the caving club happy for months. But more importantly, they also left behind a quantity of explosives: notably, a supply of anti-tank mines and relevant chemicals. One of these mines, which was the size of a quart thermos, was full of TNT. The Mendip Caving Club used these explosives to open up new entrances to caves, one of which is named after Rodney Pearce, Rod's Pot, and is a favourite among cavers worldwide today.

Rosemary Farrow was nine when the engineers built the aerodrome at Raydon in Suffolk, with its living quarters, hospital, and the like, in the village of Great Wenham where she lived. A few weeks before D-Day it was decreed that all adults in the village should have a pass to enable them to get home. Rosemary was very ill with jaundice at the time, so her mother had to have a home visit. When one of the American sergeants heard of this, he went back to camp and brought the little girl fresh orange juice and other things to improve her diet and health.

On the night before D-Day, passage in and out of the village was stopped even to those with passes. The Home Guard platoon, including Rosemary's father, were out on patrol that night, and were refused re-entry to their own village even though they were in uniform. So the platoon retreated back across a field and came in via the allotments, undetected.

At Litton Cheney in Dorset the father of Olivia Birchall was the headmaster of the small village school, and the family lived in the adjoining schoolhouse. Nissen huts were built on wasteland next to the school, to accommodate American troops who arrived before D-Day. 'Quite an event for the quiet village,' she recalls, 'especially for us living next door, with no other dwellings in the lane.'

The first contingent of soldiers quickly made themselves known to the family, popping round casually for a friendly chat. One or two from the cookhouse would appear from time to time bearing freshly cooked ring-doughnuts, which Olivia and her sister ate with gusto. Although a smallish affair, the camp had its own movie theatre and the villagers were afforded free access to films, bringing the likes of Bing Crosby and Frank Sinatra to rural Dorset.

Although the Americans were only there for a comparatively short time, Olivia remembers units changing several times, as each group departed for Europe in turn. 'At some stage,' she says, 'one of the units included a band or orchestra and several of the wives of these men stayed two or three nights with us at the schoolhouse, just before their husbands went overseas.' Unfortunately, they were later informed that the vessel carrying this particular group had been sunk.

At many locations in the south-west, preparations to accept the invasion force began as early as 1942. For instance, as a boy Jack Buzza's favourite walk on a Sunday afternoon with his grandmother was to Devil's Arch in Cornwall to pick wild flowers and gather a bag or two of kindling wood for the fire. Near Devil's Arch was a large country mansion called Pencalenick, which in 1942 became the headquarters of the 1st and 5th Engineer Special Brigades of the American Army. After 1944, US officers were based in the house, while other ranks were accommodated in tents, both in the grounds and nearby woods. Everywhere vehicles and equipment were being stockpiled, ready for loading into barges being assembled by engineers at Boscawen Park, down by the river Fal, about a mile out of Truro. On his regular walks Jack was able to observe the build-up at Pencalenick as it developed.

He remembers hundreds of these barges moored, not only in the Fal itself, but also in the Tresillian, and any other rivers and creeks along the courses of these two rivers that were big enough to conceal and camouflage them from enemy aircraft. Previously Jack had enjoyed fishing down the river in the boat of a Malpas gentleman called Sam Scoble, but suddenly both fishing and rowing were banned. The tight security surrounding Pencalenick wasn't merely to protect the barges, but because many senior officers were using it to prepare and plan elements of the invasion, including General Eisenhower himself: even Winston Churchill paid a visit. More top brass working on invasion plans used another mansion called Tulimar on the road to Falmouth.

At Turnaware Bar, not far from Truro, American engineers built a concrete road down to the water's edge, enabling their tanks and lorries to be driven straight on to the invasion barges. Jack also recalls that the *Smuggler's Inn* was being used by US troops, but it was very heavily guarded, and he never found out what was going on there.

On the other side of Truro at Treliske Manor, which is now a prep school, many black soldiers were stationed while being employed in this construction work. Jack came into contact with many of them while working at nearby Alma Farm at weekends and during holidays, as they would help with hay making, potato picking and corn harvesting.

'Just before D-Day,' he explains, 'all Pencalenick was emptied of troops and I remember seeing great holes dug in the lawns.' Jack suggests that these holes were used to bury hundreds of tons of equipment, perhaps even entire Jeeps!

At Paignton in Devon, John Gale and his father had good cause to remember the effect of the build-up of traffic before D-Day on those who relied on using the roads for their employment. As a ten-year-old living in Torquay, John would accompany his father on his bread delivery round. His father had served in both world wars but, after being medically discharged from the army, had returned to his pre-war employer who ran a bakery and owned several outlets. Part of Mr Gale's job was to deliver to these shops and, on the Saturday before D-Day, everything went as normal until they reached their final point at Preston. On reaching Seaway Road, the traffic lights were switched off and a police constable was directing the traffic. After making his delivery Mr Gale attempted to return to Torquay but was stopped by the officer who told him that the road was closed and they would have to wait for a while, as a large troop convoy was expected. The time was around 10.30a.m.

John and his father waited for a while but as Mr Gale still had a lot more work to do that day, he decided that, as he knew the area well, he could negotiate the back roads to Torquay. They set off, initially in the opposite direction, but on arriving at a small crossroads they were stopped again, this time by an officious special constable, who wouldn't let them pass. So it was back to square one.

On returning to the main road they pulled in and parked. A few trucks passed but nothing of any consequence. Then towards lunchtime a small convoy appeared, in which the trucks were quite widely spaced. Mr Gale had an idea. At a point when the trucks were stationary, he edged into the convoy, hoping to drive off with them when they got going again. Sitting in the back of the truck immediately in front was a young black soldier. He beckoned the young John across to him, and when he went over to see what the man wanted, he handed him two enormous oranges. 'Gold dust!' John recalls.

Needless to say the plan failed, and the couple were hauled out of the convoy. They didn't return home until late that evening: the expected convoy had failed to materialise.

Bernard Peters recalls that around Truro, where there was a massive influx of troops, the roads were little better than B roads, resulting in traffic jams and many 'smack-ups'. Jeeps and command cars were driven at high speed around the narrow Cornish lanes by what the locals termed 'the mad Yanks'. Large steel GMC's, 3-tonners almost as wide as the road itself, would be driven hell for leather by young men with no knowledge of small farm lanes, hemmed in by high hedges. Bernard considers the black Americans to have been the worst, throwing caution to the wind. They were 'quite reckless and mad;' he states, 'the white GIs only a little better.'

Time and time again drivers got lost. Coming up out of Falmouth, one GI driver looked at the sign for Mabe and said, 'What do they mean May Be half a mile: don't they goddam know?'

D-Day and lasting impressions

Finally the day had arrived, and the tens of thousands of American soldiers who had poured into the West Country were about to embark on what would prove to be, debatably, the single most important day of the entire 20th century. The GIs flooded into ports all along the south coast, and central to their invasion plan was the town of Weymouth, where Des Fry had worked alongside the US Navy since 1943.

Des had already witnessed many training exercises, including the disaster at Slapton Sands, but this time it was the real thing. 'Towards the end of May,' he writes, 'it was all taking shape, no more exercises, disastrous or otherwise, this was what the whole world was waiting for. Portland Harbour was overflowing with landing ships of all sizes and shapes.'

Tanks and heavy armour trundled through the town, their destination being the huge vehicle park that had been bulldozed out of Chesil Beach to the west of Portland. Here they waited to be loaded aboard the ships. Meanwhile a shuttle of army lorries were disgorging countless numbers of American GIs at the sluice garden end of Greenhill Beach, opposite what is now the entrance to the Lodmoor Country Park. On arrival they were fed doughnuts and coffee, before being sent to join the queue of assault troops that stretched all along Weymouth sea front. As they arrived at the old Skee-Ball building, which jutted out over the sands from the Prom, opposite the middle section of Alexandra Gardens, they were six abreast and sandwiched between two rows of barbed wire, one on the seaward side of the Prom, the other on the roadside. The roadside barrier was interspersed every 100 metres or so by American military policemen and other sentries.

On arrival at staging posts in Alexandra Gardens, the men were issued with an inflatable life-belt. Their mood was noticeably more sombre than that of their predecessors who a month earlier had queued here, before taking part in the exercise at Slapton Sands.

At a signal from the officer in charge of embarkation, each group of GIs would double across to the temporary landing stage, positioned at the Ferry Steps. Also at this time, two canvas enclosures appeared on the sea front, their purpose being a mystery to everyone, as indeed they were to Des until the day following the invasion, when returning bodies revealed them to be temporary mortuaries.

Dave Ford, who grew up at Underhill on the island of Portland, also recalls the build up of men and machines on Chesil Beach, saying: 'A wide stretch of the beach at the end of Ferrybridge was carved out by great bulldozers, the likes of which had never been seen before. This was a parking area for the convoys that gathered before going aboard the landing craft at Castletown.'

The local children would walk the two miles to see the waiting troops, and were literally showered with candy and coins for their trouble. Soldiers would place blankets on the ground and play crap/poker. But they only seemed to play with notes, either their own dollars or British pound or ten-shilling notes. There was little point in being weighed down with British coinage, and they would throw it to the expectant throng of local kids. 'Being thrown a half crown in those days was a fortune for a small boy,' explains Dave. The problem was that, as sweets were rationed, there was little for them to spend their new found wealth on.

As D-Day neared, more and more troops arrived and tents were actually put up along the pavements of Chesil with steel pegs hammered into the asphalt to secure the guide ropes.

Graham Toms says of the Americans who were stationed around Yeovil: 'Then suddenly the majority of them were gone. The fields were empty of vehicles and men, as they had left the night before to go to Weymouth, Southampton and other ports to be part of the task force for Omaha Beach. We never saw the like of it again. Several died in the landings and I can recall seeing the hospital trains full of wounded men being transported to various hospitals throughout the area. There were two American hospitals in the Yeovil area at Lufton camp and Houndstone camp. At that time I was part of the Grass Royal School Concert Party and I can remember that after a week of entertaining parents and staff we were transported by army trucks to give a performance to the wounded at the two camps. Perhaps some of them were the same men that I, with my parents, had seen waiting to depart at Weymouth, thousands of them filling the promenade and joking with the on-lookers, tossing them their English money.'

Then it was D-Day itself, 6 June 1944, and everything was deadly quiet. Des Fry, who the day before had seen the many ships waiting in Portland Harbour, cycled down to Weymouth seafront on the way to work at the American Naval base, at 7.30a.m. He remembers that the sea was calm, the sun shining, the birds twittering, but in the harbour not a single ship lay at anchor, and the GIs had all disappeared from along the seafront.

At last, on entering the main gate of the base, he met a solitary American sentry, with carbine slung over his shoulder, and he felt somehow glad to see him. After entry, the base and workshops also appeared deserted, and he recalls seeing no more than two Sea Bees during his progress. However, this semblance of tranquillity was shattered at around 8.30a.m. when the sky over the town filled with aircraft appearing from inland to head out towards France over White Nose Cliffs. This thick line of aircraft, many towing gliders, continued for much of the day.

Neither Des nor Alf accomplished much work that day, as they sat glued to the wireless with their few remaining American buddies waiting for news, along with people throughout Weymouth and indeed the whole of Britain.

The next day, 7 June, the lines of GIs returned to the Promenade, relentlessly moving along to reinforce the beach-heads; this was to continue for months, together with more armoured vehicles to be shipped from Portland. Also on that day Weymouth saw the first casualties return and the canvas mortuaries pressed into their grim service. The days, weeks and months following D-Day were all taken up with ferrying men and machines to the Normandy beaches. So the columns of GIs remained a familiar sight on the Promenade for some time to come.

The father of Mrs B. Grant, who was a liaison officer with the Army Pay Corps at the time of D-Day worked from an office at the *Normandy Hotel* in Boscombe, on the Dorset coast, which had been taken over by the Army for the duration of the war. He would often walk across the cliffs and tell the family of the large build-up of ships in the area around Bournemouth. Opposite their house in Granville Road was a garage, which at about the same time was taken over to accommodate American troops. Suddenly, the soldiers were confined to the garage and none of the children were allowed access to them. Then one morning in June they were gone, and that evening her father

152 Some of the thousands of American soldiers who marched through Torquay on the way to board their landing craft for the D-Day invasion, watched by a local 'bobby'. (Photo: courtesy of Alan Heather/Torquay Museum)

153 A member of the 303rd Bomb Group at the Cambridge Military Cemetery, standing over the original wooden marker for 1Lt John J McGarry Jr killed in action on 9 April 1944. His body was later returned to the USA. (Photo: courtesy of 303rd Bomb Group Association)

returned from work with the news that all the ships waiting around Bournemouth had disappeared as well.

For most people, especially those in the West Country, who had experienced a couple of months of intense American occupation, their association with their cousins from over the pond had come to an end. From D-Day until the end of the war in Europe, in May 1945, although thousands more passed through Britain on their way to the European battlefields, the 'Friendly Invasion' was effectively drawing to its conclusion.

In much of East Anglia, the GIs stayed a little longer, still utilising their airbases to wreak havoc on Hitler's declining forces across the Channel. But even here, many of the aircraft and men moved to the continent, to continue the war from bases in France and, later, other parts of liberated Europe. This left only skeleton crews of men back in England, and eventually it was time even for them to leave.

The last memory Jean Angel has of the airmen from Ridgewell was joining other villagers at the railway station to see them off, and eating sticky, sugary doughnuts on the way home.

GIs of the 97th Bomb Group vacated the Polebrook airbase in lorries, passing through the village of Warmington near Oundle, where Rosemary Robson grew up. Here many village residents lined the road and waved them off. As they passed the American airmen threw sweets to the children.

This book has tried to give an unbiased point of view, and has shown the negative side of the 'Friendly Invasion' as well as the positive, but what are the lasting impressions that the Americans left on the British public.

Vera Anderson says: 'We are now all old people, but all the same I am so glad I did not miss those years. Everyone helped and shared what little we had and it left me with so many memories. When the Americans came to England, it was a huge boost for us all and I am so proud to have known them.' This sentiment is reinforced by Mrs J. Tombs, who lived in Bury St Edmunds and says, 'Although I am 71 now I have vivid memories of them – they were nice guys and brought us hope in those grey days.'

Bernard Peters recalls the aftermath of D-Day on the Truro area. Suddenly the river Fal was open again, so was Boscawen Park, and gradually the beaches were cleared of mines. At Perranporth the Fire Brigade used their hoses to sweep the mined areas, the force of the jet exploding the mines buried there. The steel scaffolding poles along the beach at Pendower were dismantled, before which children had to negotiate barbed wire and steel to get a swim. Also a French minesweeper, sunk by the Germans, was available to play on at low tide.

The Yanks didn't take everything with them: various tools and steel mesh sheets were left behind on the mud. Bernard became the proud owner of a large metal sign from a GMC lorry wing. It was in the shape

154 Sally, the American Red Cross Entertainment Officer in Devizes, packed up and ready to return home in September 1945. (Photo: courtesy of Elsie Lewis)

155 *SS Queen Elizabeth* arriving at New York on 31 August 1945, with 14,860 returning troops aboard. (Photo: copyright 486th Bomb Group Association)

of the American eagle with wings out-stretched, its head like a pointed rocket. The Cornish mine shafts took lots of unwanted equipment, even damaged bicycles, propane bottles, and expensive brass pressure gauges.

As time went by surplus war stock – especially Jeeps, command cars, Hillman utilities, GMC lorries, petrol cans and associated gear – went on sale at Ministry of Supply auctions. Vast amounts ended up in Army and Navy shops.

At the end of the day, America and Britain were political allies and their servicemen had little say in how, or why the war was fought. They were merely the people expected to fight it on the ground, on the sea, or in the air and, if duty required, they were expected to lay down their lives. Most British soldiers and American GIs believed that the Second World War was a just war, and were indeed willing to make the ultimate sacrifice to preserve the values they believed in. But at the same time, most longed for the war to end, so they could go home to their wives, children, and the people they loved.

Cartoonist George Rarey came to England in 1943 as a fighter pilot. While he was here his new bride Betty Lou gave birth to their son Damon, and his letters home were full of humour, hope and love. His sense of duty comes across very strongly, as does his desire to help the allies defeat their enemies, but at the same time his letters are underlined with a longing for the war to end, so that he can return to his family and enjoy a life of peace.

George Rarey was killed in combat over France a few weeks after D-Day, so he never got to know his son. His final letter home, dated 26 June 1944, is a beautiful and poignant reminder of the reasons why ordinary people go to war and are prepared to kill and die, in order to protect everything they hold dear.

> Dear Betty Lou – I don't care for this war – I want you and Damon and the life of our choosing. I want to worry about the bills – ho! ho! – and mow the lawn and make kites and stuff for the demon and his friends. I want to see you and kiss you every day of my life – I want to beef about your silly hats and tell you how lovely you are. I've got all these things to do and time's a wastin' – I ain't getting any younger, neither! So let's get the war over –okay.

Index

References which relate to illustrations only are given in **bold**